RENEWALS 458-4574

DATE

WITHDRAWN
UTSA LIBRARIES

The American Research University
from World War II to World Wide Web

THE CLARK KERR LECTURES ON THE
ROLE OF HIGHER EDUCATION IN SOCIETY

1. *The American Research University from World War II to World Wide Web: Governments, the Private Sector, and the Emerging Meta-University*, by Charles M. Vest

The American Research University
from World War II
to World Wide Web

Governments, the Private Sector, and
the Emerging Meta-University

Charles M. Vest

UNIVERSITY OF CALIFORNIA PRESS

Berkeley   Los Angeles   London

CENTER FOR STUDIES IN HIGHER EDUCATION

Berkeley

Library
University of Texas
at San Antonio

The Center for Studies in Higher Education at the University of California, Berkeley, is a multidisciplinary research and policy center on higher education oriented to California, the nation, and comparative international issues. CSHE promotes discussion among university leaders, government officials, and academics; assists policy making by providing a neutral forum for airing contentious issues; and keeps the higher education world informed of new initiatives and proposals. The Center's research aims to inform current debate about higher education policy and practice.

University of California Press, one of the most distinguished university presses in the United States, enriches lives around the world by advancing scholarship in the humanities, social sciences, and natural sciences. Its activities are supported by the UC Press Foundation and by philanthropic contributions from individuals and institutions. For more information, visit www.ucpress.edu.

University of California Press
Berkeley and Los Angeles, California

University of California Press, Ltd.
London, England

© 2007 by The Regents of the University of California

Library of Congress Cataloging-in-Publication Data

Vest, Charles M.
    The American research university from World War II to world wide web : governments, the private sector, and the emerging meta-university / Charles M. Vest.
        p.   cm. — (Clark Kerr lectures on the role of higher education in society ; 1)
    Includes bibliographical references and index.
    ISBN 978-0-520-25253-0 (cloth : alk. paper)
    1. Research institutes—United States—History—20th century.   2. Science—Study and teaching—United States—History—20th century.   3. Technology—Study and teaching (Higher)—United States—History—20th century.   4. Universities and colleges—Research—United States.   5. Universities and colleges—Economic aspects—United States.   I. Title.

Q180.U5V47   2007
001.4'0973—dc22   2006029086

Manufactured in the United States of America

16   15   14   13   12   11   10   09   08   07
10   9   8   7   6   5   4   3   2   1

This book is printed on New Leaf EcoBook 50, a 100% recycled fiber of which 50% is de-inked post-consumer waste, processed chlorine-free. EcoBook 50 is acid-free and meets the minimum requirements of ANSI/ASTM D5634–01 (*Permanence of Paper*).

Library
University of Texas
at San Antonio

This book is dedicated to
Mary Louise, Robert, and Ameri.

New frontiers of the mind are before us, and if they are pioneered with the same vision, boldness, and drive with which we have waged this war we can create a fuller and more fruitful employment and a fuller and more fruitful life.

President Franklin D. Roosevelt to Vannevar Bush
November 17, 1944

If ability, and not the circumstance of family fortune, determines who shall receive higher education, then we shall be assured of constantly improving quality at every level of scientific activity.

Vannevar Bush to President Harry S. Truman
July 5, 1945

May we now use every ability we have to communicate to build a society in which mutual respect, understanding and peace occur at all scales, between people and between nations.

Tim Berners-Lee, Japan Prize Lecture
2002

CONTENTS

Acknowledgments

XI

Introduction

I

1. Governments and Universities:
The Roles and Influences of the
Public Sector in Higher Education

5

2. Industry, Philanthropy, and Universities:
The Roles and Influences of the Private Sector in
Higher Education

37

3. Openness: Education, Research, and
Scholarly Communication in an Age of
Globalization and Terrorism

70

4. The Emerging Global Meta-University: Higher
Education and Scholarship in the Age of the Internet

91

Notes

111

Index

117

ACKNOWLEDGMENTS

I want to thank several present and past colleagues at MIT, each of whom contributed something of direct value to the writing of this book: Hal Abelson, Larry Bacow, Bob Brown, Jack Crowley, Jesus del Alamo, Alice Gast, Paul Gray, Danielle Guichard-Ashbrook, Elizabeth Hicks, Stan Hudson, Marilee Jones, Vijay Kumar, Steve Lerman, Tom Magnanti, Anne Margulies, Laura Mersky, Penny Rosser, Rob Scott, Thane Scott, Constantine Simonides, Barbara Stowe, Glenn Strehle, Tia Tilson, Kathryn Willmore, Ann Wolpert, and Dick Yue. Dan Atkins and Jim Duderstadt of the University of Michigan were very helpful. Several people at the University of California were helpful to this effort: at Berkeley, Bob Birgeneau, John Douglass, Irwin Feller, Jud King, and Karl Pister; and at Riverside, Susan Hackwood. Paul Brest and Mike Smith of the Hewlett Foundation and Bill Bowen, Ira Fuchs, and Kevin Guthrie of the Mellon Foundation and Ithaka contributed in many ways to the content of chapter 4, as did David Wylie of Utah State University. John Vaughn of the Association of American Universities, Sandra Baum of the College Board, and Morty Shapiro of Williams College were helpful in understanding certain data relating to financial aid.

Introduction

This volume is based on three lectures I delivered at the University of California as the 2005 Clark Kerr Lecturer on the Role of Higher Education in Society. This lectureship and the encouragement and support of the members and staff of the Center for Studies in Higher Education at the University of California, Berkeley, provided an extraordinary opportunity for me to organize and present some personal observations and opinions about American higher education garnered during forty-five years as a student, professor, and administrator in both public and private research universities.

I am particularly pleased that this work is presented in honor of Clark Kerr. There is no one whose legacy in higher education, or in our understanding of higher education in the twentieth century, exceeds that of Clark Kerr. Kerr was a doer and builder, not just an observer and theoretician. He was the principal architect of the 1960 California Master Plan for Higher Education. This framework still governs the state's three systems of higher education (the University of California, the California State Universities, and the Community Colleges); determines which students are eligible for each of these systems; and guarantees access for those who are qualified.

Kerr's shadow looms large over the American educational landscape. His understanding of the emergence of the *multiversity*—as he famously termed it in his 1963 Godkin Lectures at Harvard—crystallized our view of the tectonic changes that occurred in U.S. research universities at the middle of the twentieth century.

Perspectives and experiences change with time and over generations. In 1963 Kerr described the rapid transformation of our research universities into something new and different. Campuses sprawled intellectually even as they sprawled physically across the landscape of state after state. As our universities evolved, they developed a complex web of purposes, which created increasing tensions between the goals of societal utility and academic purity.

In the same year that Kerr articulated this insight, and much more, in the Godkin Lectures, I graduated from West Virginia University and immediately headed to Ann Arbor to begin my graduate studies in mechanical engineering at the University of Michigan. What to Kerr, as a leader of his generation, was a surprising new incarnation of the American research university was for me a given. Michigan, MIT, Berkeley, Caltech, and Stanford were magnetic attractors to a young engineering student who was truly a child of the Sputnik era.

My strong attraction to these schools largely resulted from what has been termed the *engineering science revolution*. This revolution was spawned primarily by faculty at MIT, who, building on their experiences in the MIT Radiation Laboratory during World War II, created a radically different way to practice and teach engineering. The "Rad Lab" had brought together a remarkable group of scientists and engineers to rapidly develop battle-ready radar systems using concepts and elements invented by the British. Many believe that radar was at least as instrumental in the Allied victory as were the bombs developed at the better-known laboratory at Los Alamos. Another towering legacy of the Rad Lab work was a new world of engineering education, built more on a solid foundation of science than on traditional macroscopic phenomenology, charts, handbooks, and codes. The new engineering science, which relied on intense research and required an entirely new panoply of textbooks and laboratories, drove change in a broad range of fields, among them the space program, defense, transportation, telecommunications, computing, and medicine. Its assimilation into curricula was accelerated by the 1955 report of the American Society for Engineering Education's Committee on Evaluation of Engineering Curricula.[1]

MIT, under engineering dean Gordon Brown, and Stanford, under provost Frederic Terman, were the first to adopt this new approach to engineering education, and Berkeley, Wisconsin, Michigan, Illinois, and other institutions soon followed and became strong contributors to it. This corner of the emerging multiversity was very attractive and exciting. What a joy it was to pursue my engineering education in this heady environment, and also to have friends who were students of medicine, law, history, chemistry, mathematics, social work, education, and philosophy. How remarkable it was to be on a campus with endless opportunities to attend world-class musical events, to visit the art museum, and to attend lectures by the most influential scholars or practitioners from every discipline imaginable.

In short, as a student I learned and worked at the new boundaries of academic engineering, and yet still felt very much a part of the great, centuries-old traditions and values of academia. These two aspects of the multiversity did not, and still do not, strike me as inconsistent. Rather, the multiversity as I experienced it was a noble and enabling place. What appeared to many to be sources of tension, cross-purposes, and potential conflicts of values and interests were for me a great web or mosaic to be savored and celebrated. This was what I expected a university to be. And, despite the passage of over forty years, it still is.

In this volume I explore four dimensions of the American research university as I have come to understand them. The first concerns the contemporary relationship of universities with governments—federal, state, and local. The second deals with the roles and influences on our universities of the private sector—industry and philanthropists. The third explores the importance of the open, international flow of people and ideas across our campus boundaries, and the ways in which such openness is challenged in an era when global terrorism has reached America's shores. The fourth concerns the role of the Internet and World Wide Web in scholarship and higher education, and what I consider to be an evolving global *meta-university*.

ONE

Governments and Universities

The Roles and Influences of the
Public Sector in Higher Education

MY PERSONAL (UNIVERSITY) JOURNEY

In 1990, when it was announced that I had been elected president of MIT, I received a letter from one of my Michigan colleagues, Paul McCracken, a distinguished economist and former chair of the Council of Economic Advisors. Here is the text of his letter in its entirety:

> Dear Chuck,
>
>> Boy from West Virginia becomes president of MIT.
>> The American Dream.
>
> Sincerely,
> Paul

That brief note, in my view, encapsulates what is best about American higher education—we create opportunity. That is our mission. That is our business. That is first and foremost what society expects of us.

Great public universities like Berkeley and Michigan have a special role in that mission of creating opportunity. It is captured in the motto coined for the University of Michigan in the nineteenth century: "An uncommon education for the common man." Now, of course, we have arguments about who we are creating opportunity for, and why, and how. But it remains the fundamental mission.

Universities, especially research-intensive universities, are increasingly viewed—by themselves and by others—as institutions that create opportunity not just for individuals, but also for states, regions, nations, or industries by virtue of the economic impact of the knowledge and the educated men and women they produce. This form of opportunity creation, driven largely by research activities, is more complicated than that of providing an uncommon education for the common person, and support for it is less uniformly agreed upon. But I believe it is an important and wonderful part of our mission as well.

My experiences as an undergraduate at West Virginia University; as a graduate student, professor, and administrator at the University of Michigan; as a visiting faculty member at Stanford; and as president of MIT have left me with a profound respect for American higher education and a deep appreciation for the opportunities I have received, helped to develop, and observed.

WHAT MAKES AMERICAN
HIGHER EDUCATION EXCELLENT?

We in the American academy sometimes get so wrapped up in our modest tribulations and so upset by the discrepancies between our ideals and some realities that we lose sight of how fundamentally good we are at what we do. The governments that support much of our work frequently appear to understand our importance less and less, and they sometimes seem to criticize us more than to support us. And there are many critics abroad these days to whom we must pay attention. But be that as it may, the rest of the world recognizes our essential greatness and the beauty and effectiveness of the opportunities and success we bring to our nation and world. Educators in countless countries work diligently to learn our ways and means and to emulate them within their own contexts. As is disclosed in study after study, ranking after ranking, and through that greatest of all compliments—emulation—we really are the proverbial "envy of the world."

This was driven home for me a few years ago when I conversed over dinner with the rector of Humboldt University of Berlin. He looked at me and in all seriousness asked if I had any advice regarding how the U.S. research-university model could be successfully transplanted to Germany. The irony, of course, is that in the nineteenth century the United States, and specifically the Johns Hopkins University, imported the concept of the research university from Humboldt!

This leads me to suggest some fundamental reasons why U.S. higher education continues to be excellent, effective, and well respected by our international peers.

- A diverse array of institutions, ranging from small liberal-arts colleges to Ivy League schools to the great land-grant universities, provides a wealth of environments and opportunities for students to select a school that best matches their needs and capabilities. This diversity also brings with it a wide range of funding sources, which are not available to the state-operated universities that dominate in many other countries.

- New assistant professors have the freedom to choose what they teach and the topics of research and scholarship they pursue. They are not subservient or apprenticed to senior professors, so they bring to our institutions a constant flow of new ideas, passions, and approaches.

- In our research universities we meaningfully weave together teaching and research. This too brings freshness, intensity, and constant renewal.

- We welcome students, scholars, and faculty from other countries. They bring a defining quality of intellectual and cultural richness to our institutions.

- There is an implicit national science and technology policy that recognizes support of frontier research in our universities as an important responsibility of the federal government. This policy is intended to provide financial support to researchers, based on their merit in a competitive marketplace of ideas. Funding for infrastructure is attached to grants and contracts, and therefore flows to the researchers with the most meritorious ideas and track records.

- There is a tradition of individual philanthropy through which our alumni and others support our colleges and universities financially. Financial aid derived from their gifts enables talented students from families of modest means to attend even the most costly schools. Tax laws encourage such donations.

- There is open competition for faculty and students. Such inter-institutional competition, though it may be the bane of academic administrators' daily lives, drives excellence.

- An oft-overlooked and initially unique characteristic of American universities is their broad and deep commitment to public service. This is most clearly manifested in the land-grant tradition that brought agriculture and engineering into our public universities and developed mechanisms for transferring the fruits of study and research in these fields to America's farms and industries. Today a commitment to public service permeates essentially all segments of the university community and has led to strong interactions with business, industry, and government. This is true in nationally oriented private universities, and it is especially the case in most public universities that are linked to state, regional, and local industrial needs.

These factors are primarily structural—matters of public will, public policy, and, indeed, public financial resources. Other nations could profitably consider these factors, integrate them into their own cultural and political context, and perhaps improve upon them. Intelligence, curiosity, and creativity have no national boundaries. Great universities based on this residential, research-intensive model can and do arise anywhere in the world. As demonstrated by the enormous success and impact of the Indian Institutes of Technology, which were established in the 1960s, higher education can leap forward very rapidly.

PUBLIC/PRIVATE—
GEOGRAPHIC DISTRIBUTION

In order to keep myself refreshed, relevant, and experienced, I take advantage of one of the most cherished perquisites of an academic career—the sabbatical leave. Indeed, I go on sabbatical regularly—once every thirty years. During my last sabbatical, in 1974, my wife and I packed up our young children and drove across the country from Ann Arbor to Palo Alto. It was a delightful journey, covering 4,500 miles, although it would only have been about 2,000 miles as the crow flies.

One of the things I discovered is that the dominant shades of tan and gray in the landscape change as one moves west. More remarkably, the color of rabbits, chipmunks, prairie dogs, and other critters changes to match the color of the soil, rocks, and wood. I assume they do this also in Kansas, where evolution may not apply for the moment, but I didn't test that empirically.

But on a journey from east to west, the framework for higher education also changes, not by adapting to the soil color, but as a result of the slow westward movement of the population and the consequent development of social and political structures. In a nutshell, private colleges and universities, often founded with religious as well as secular objectives, dominate in the east. As one moves through the Midwest and the Great Plains, one finds the remarkable legacy of great state universities left by the land-grant acts, the Northwest Ordinance, and the commonly shared needs of earlier agrarian societies, but only a smattering of private institutions. By the time we reach California, we encounter perhaps our most refined system of state colleges and universities, as well as a modest but exquisite "second growth" of private universities.

Predictably, then, the relative role of the federal and state governments in relation to our universities also shifts and changes across the land. But I have also found that this is less and less true as time goes on—that is, there is a significant degree of convergence of structure, purpose, and funding of public and private institutions.

PUBLIC/PRIVATE—
FINANCIAL FORCES AND REACTIONS

Having now served a private institution for fifteen years and having also observed public universities by looking back to Michigan and out at others, I can summarize their financial differences succinctly: When the economy is strong and growing, the grass is greener on the other side. When the economy is weak and declining, the grass is browner on the other side.

That is to say, public and private institutions are ultimately subjected to the same economic forces, but the public universities seem to respond with greater volatility. MIT usually sees a modest but steady year-to-year growth in faculty salaries, while even the best public institutions may have zero raises one year and double-digit increases a couple of years later. And then there is the flip side—the differing nature of capital funding. At Michigan, the state legislature could often find the money for buildings, largely because of the attendant construction jobs, in years when salary budgets were hard to come by. At MIT, on the other hand, it was a hair-raising experience to orchestrate a major improvement of our campus between 1998 and 2005. We constructed about 25 percent of our current campus while the economy and equity markets skyrocketed upward at unprecedented rates and then decided that the laws of economics had not been repealed and dove downward again. Add to that the fact that Boston-area construction costs also grew at historically unprecedented rates and did not drop when the economy went south, because the famous Big Dig was a huge federal project that was not subject to the laws of free-market economics.

You too would be ready for your once-every-thirty-years sabbatical!

Although these public/private differences have persisted for three or four decades, we are converging at a greater and greater rate. I think this is driven primarily by three factors. First, we are all dependent on the federal government as the lifeblood of our research and graduate-education enterprises. Second, private giving and endowment support increasingly provides the edge of excellence in state universities. Third, the roller-coaster ride of the dot-com-era economy was so extreme that even the budgets of strong private universities whose names do not begin with *H* or *P* had to respond with uncharacteristic swings. Thus during the last two years, Caltech, MIT, and Stanford all implemented operating-budget reductions and salary freezes of one form or another in order to position themselves back onto their traditional steady but moderate growth curves.

In 1969 two-thirds of every dollar expended on the MIT campus through our operating budget came from the federal government, primarily from sponsored research. In 2004 only 36 percent of our campus operating budget came from sponsored research, of which about 60 percent was from the federal government. So, although our volume of federal research support continued to grow, and remains indispensable, it has declined dramatically as a fraction of our operating expenses.

Private support in the form of gifts, grants, and return on endowment grew from 20 percent to almost 40 percent to make up the difference. Of course, tuition has also grown, but we have worked very hard to restrain its rate of growth and to continue to raise the huge amounts required to maintain the financial-aid structure that makes MIT accessible to young men and women regardless of their financial status.

Because of the dominant role at MIT of science and engineering, both expensive disciplines, we are perhaps at the extreme in the magnitude of these shifts, at least in nonmedical fields, but the general description of a federal decline and a private increase in revenues to support our mission is still generic to private research universities. Stanford, for example, would present a similar profile. We have no state support to rely on—only tuition revenues, net of financial aid, and gifts and endowment income.

The story of Berkeley, or UCLA, or Michigan, or Illinois over forty years would be the inverse of this. On the time scale of decades, the fraction of federal research support in their operating budgets has grown dramatically—although over the last decade, outside the biomedical fields, it has generally leveled out, even as various expenses have risen. State support has generally played the role for these public institutions that endowment has played for the privates. State support has provided infrastructure and has kept tuition and fees from growing as rapidly as they might have otherwise.

Indeed, 70 percent of the University of Michigan's budget in the 1960s came from the state, with the remaining 30 percent approximately equally divided among federal research and development funds, tuition income, and private support. Today, excluding its medical center, about 31 percent of Michigan's income for operations comes from sponsored research and only 13 percent from the state.

Despite the role of state support at public universities, private funding increasingly supports the margin of excellence, large fractions of capital construction, and other special operating expenses. In fact, in 2003–04 only five of the twenty largest university endowments belonged to public universities,[1] but in the preceding year almost half of the twenty largest annual fund-raising totals were those of public universities.[2] So, in time the endowment gap between leading publics and privates will narrow. The large alumni donor bases of public universities will make this possible.

In the availability and role of federal research support and of private fund-raising, then, the leading research-intensive publics and privates look more and more alike, with some of the fiscal volatility that has characterized state universities occurring in the privates as well. But this view of convergence, while qualitatively correct, is deceptive. The reason it is deceptive is that the *scales* of public and private universities are very different. The largest endowment of a public university is the University of Texas System's $10.2 billion, and the largest private-university endowment is Harvard's $22 billion. But the University of Texas System has 160,000 students, while Harvard has 24,000 students. Thus the Texas System's endowment per student is $64,000, while that of Harvard is almost $1 million, about sixteen times that of Texas. Or to compare two other institutions of a more typical scale, the University of Michigan Ann Arbor's endowment per student is approximately $115,000, while MIT's is $570,000, about five times that of Michigan. For Berkeley or UCLA, endowment per student is on the order of $50,000.

If our national economy were to grow steadily and strongly, and the federal commitment to research and advanced education were to grow as well, I think that the public and private research universities would continue to converge in their fiscal structure, while maintaining a healthy difference in their relative size and tuition levels. But this has not been the case. First, over the past thirty years federal support of university research in virtually all areas of physical and social science and of engineering has been essentially constant in purchasing power. But during this period, the number of public institutions capable of doing excellent research and advanced education has clearly grown in both the public and private domains. Second, and far more important, a combination of decreased tax bases and societal priority has led to leveling and decline in absolute state support. The situation has varied in its severity from state to state, but the basic story is more or less the same everywhere. The likely long-term consequence of these financial realities will be growing disparities between public and private universities in factors like faculty salaries, combined with converging levels of tuition and fees.

Since 1980 faculty salaries at public universities have lost substantial ground relative to those at the privates, despite the fact that resident tuitions at public universities have grown more or less in parallel with private-university tuitions. F. King Alexander has recently studied the average difference of salaries of full professors at public and private Carnegie I research institutions, measured in constant dollars.[3] In 1980 this salary difference was 2 percent. By 1990 the public/private salary disparity had grown to 20 percent, and after peaking at 27 percent in 1995 it is about 25 percent today. During this same period, the average public-university tuition for in-state resident undergraduates was always approximately 20 percent of the average private-university tuition, and the average nonresident public-university tuition grew from 47 percent to 58 percent of the average private tuition.[4]

These overall average numbers do not present an entirely fair picture. For example, there are various differences in expectations, responsibilities, disciplinary distribution, infrastructure needs, and market forces among the professorates of these diverse universities. And because of financial aid, the actual cost of attending these public and private universities, especially for students and families in low-income brackets, is often not nearly as disparate as the tuition numbers alone imply. But all in all, the picture these financial facts paint is one of great concern.

The reaction of state universities to these fiscal realities during the next decade could well bring fundamental change to the landscape of America's higher education. One of the words most frequently spoken today by leaders of major public universities is *privatization*. Indeed, for the last twenty or thirty years leaders of public universities have frequently observed that only a small fraction of their total operating budget comes from state support. Typical current levels of state support are: 10 percent at Michigan, 13 percent at Virginia, 25 percent at Wisconsin.[5] Public presidents and chancellors frequently, and rather accurately, point out that their institutions have moved from being *state supported*, to being *state assisted*, to being *located in the state*. This, coupled with a desire to maintain or establish absolute academic excellence, invariably leads to serious consideration of becoming private.

However, there are both pragmatic and policy considerations that should lead to caution on this front. In the budget of a typical state university, the stream of funding that supports its most fundamental mission—undergraduate education—is predominantly from its state government, and most of its other revenue is not fungible. Federal or industrial support for research, for example, cannot be used for other purposes. Even very large fractions of private gifts and endowments are restricted to specific purposes.

When speaking of privatizing a university, one must immediately ask, "How much endowment would I need to replace my state support?" On average, universities expend about 5 percent of the market value of their endowment each year, so the necessary incremental endowment would be approximately twenty times the annual state appropriation received by the university. For UCLA, this would be about $12.2 billion; for Berkeley, about $10.2 billion; and for Michigan, about $6.4 billion.[6] These are very substantial amounts of money, and they account for the universities' operating budgets only; they do not account for capital investments by the state.

The issue of scale must also be addressed. Typical enrollments of the larger private universities, in round numbers, are 24,000 (Harvard), 19,000 (Stanford), and 23,000 (Penn). Among leading state universities, enrollments typically are about 50 percent larger—for example, 32,000 (Berkeley), 37,000 (UCLA), 39,000 (Michigan), and 27,000 (North Carolina, Chapel Hill).[7] I suspect that to a large extent the private enrollments are set points established by fundamental economic forces. Indeed, if one considers private colleges that do not engage substantially in sponsored research activities or have professional schools, enrollments are an order of magnitude smaller still.

One must be cautious when speaking seriously of privatizing large public universities. Caution, however, need not be an excuse to maintain the status quo. The most likely outcome of all this is that the existing trends will continue—that is, more or less privatized professional schools or other specialized units will exist within public universities, while their core mission and much of their infrastructure will remain largely state supported. A good example is that the University of Virginia's law and business schools are now becoming private, emulating to a degree the long-standing precedent of Cornell, with its public and private components. But it also is not out of the question that a small handful of leading public universities might negotiate with their states for conditions under which they could become truly private, with the state perhaps creating some of the necessary endowment in return for agreements—for example, about the number of state citizens who will be educated.

Beyond the purely financial considerations of privatization, there is an even more important matter of policy—the nature of the social contract between the states and their universities. State universities were established above all else to create opportunity for young citizens to advance themselves, and to strengthen the states' economies and general welfare. They have served this purpose admirably over the years. When contemplating changes such as privatization, universities and state governments must address these fundamental questions: In the future, will we still offer a great opportunity to the citizens of our state? Will access to our campuses still be sufficient? Will we offer degrees in an appropriately broad range of humanities, arts, sciences, and professional disciplines?

James Garland has suggested an interesting model by which a state's public universities might become private while retaining a significant public-policy role for the state's government. According to this model, the universities would become independent private corporations, and the state legislature would convert its annual higher-education appropriation into a fund to provide need-based scholarships to state residents admitted to them.[8]

Over time, as the populations of many states have grown, certain public universities have become excellent institutions encompassing a broad array of research, scholarship, and professional education that has enabled them to provide "uncommon educations for common men and women" and to offer a wide range of opportunity for the citizens of the state. World-class excellence among such so-called flagship universities has also led to more cosmopolitan student bodies and to greater catalytic roles in state economies. These institutions have become great sources of justifiable pride for their states. But it is a pride that often seems transient.

When I was growing up in West Virginia during the 1950s, that state funded the establishment of a new hospital for the university's medical school by levying a small, targeted tax on all soft drinks sold in the state. The population felt a sense of purpose and great pride of ownership of this university and medical school. In a similar vein, Americans of that era were very aware of the transformative nature of the GI Bill. Hopefully my nostalgia will be forgiven, but it would be wonderful if this widespread spirit of pride and purpose in public higher education could be regained today.

PUBLIC/PRIVATE—
EXCELLENCE IN WHAT AND FOR WHOM

There has always been, and always will be, a tension between the federal and state governments that provide financial support for colleges and universities and the faculties and administrations of those institutions regarding the definitions and roles of excellence and access. To oversimplify the matter, governments tend to have a more utilitarian view of universities than do their faculties and administrations. Academic excellence as we understand it can be thought to be somewhat at odds with the certain populist philosophies that frequently dominate state legislatures and/or boards of regents.

Numbers of nonresident students, selection criteria for admission, tuition and fees, the allocation of financial aid, the balance of undergraduate education with graduate and professional training, and the overall size of student bodies are perennial matters of debate and tension among state governments, taxpayers, and university administrators, faculty, and students. Difficult as these matters are, they usually get resolved in due course through reasonably orderly political and administrative processes. But in our times, nothing has been so bitterly contested as the role of race, and diversity more broadly, in the admission of students, and it has not been resolved through orderly political and administrative processes. Rather, it has frequently led to acrimonious conflicts and has followed multiple pathways, including public referenda and Supreme Court cases. It has torn at the heart and soul of our populations and institutions.

Our seeming inability to resolve this admission issue and the even deeper problems in our society and K–12 system that lie beneath it has left us with a perverse correlation between race and educational access and success. According to the National Center for Public Policy and Higher Education, "In 2000, whites ages 25 to 64 were twice as likely to have a bachelor's degree as African-Americans, and almost three times as likely as Hispanics/Latinos." Worse still, this gap is growing.[9]

Arguments over diversity in public universities are laden with historical legacies, value systems, political ideologies, schemas for social good, legal technicalities, views of academic excellence, attempts to balance individual and societal benefits, and assumptions about evaluating quality. These arguments are frequently spiced with mean-spiritedness as well. But they are of central importance to the future of our states and nation.

I believe that the majority of those who engage in this debate share a common view of how the world should be—namely, a world with a color-blind society that has institutions capable of evaluating each university applicant on an absolute, ordered scale of merit. The argument then should be a mutually respectful debate over how to reach that goal. But that is rarely the case.

One camp in the debate over diversity and affirmative action assumes that we have reached—or should pretend to have reached—a color-blind world, and that by lining up a few metrics like SAT scores and grades, we can fairly and objectively order the candidates and select the students to be admitted to the freshman classes of public institutions. The problem is that race still matters in America, and we are not capable of comparing each applicant to all the others on a simple but meaningful, quantitative, absolute basis.

My own view of these matters is that of an engineer who believes that problems should be directly addressed and effectively solved. It is the view of one who grew up in a border state between North and South, attended segregated public schools until ninth grade, and has spent a career as a student, teacher, and administrator in public and private universities. It is based on observation and experience, passionately held, and legally supported by the U.S. Supreme Court in the *Bakke* and University of Michigan admission cases.

Simply put, I believe that we as universities must preserve the legal right and moral authority to consider race as one of many factors in college and university admissions and in other programs and dimensions of life and learning on our campuses. Indeed, this is essential to effectively pursue a goal that is stated in MIT's mission statement:

> MIT is dedicated to providing its students with an education that combines rigorous academic study and the excitement of discovery with the support and intellectual stimulation of a diverse campus community.

To implement this mission at MIT, we first establish which of our ten thousand applicants cross a high bar of quality, based on measures such as grades, test scores, and class rank—regardless of their race or of any other characteristics. Then we make difficult, subjective choices from among those applicants who crossed the high bar by assessing as best we can the whole person. Race is one of many factors considered at this stage to build an understanding of who each person is, and the context in which he or she has demonstrated accomplishment, creativity, and drive. One of the consequences of this approach is that at MIT today our undergraduates are 44 percent women, 6 percent African American, 12 percent Hispanic American, 1 percent Native American—a student body that is remarkably diverse in so many other dimensions as well. I believe that this serves our nation's future well by providing opportunity to young men and women of remarkable academic talent, and by helping to build a future scientific and engineering workforce and leadership that reasonably reflects our population and its spectrum of cultures.

This is in stark contrast to my early years as an engineering educator. When I began my career as a teaching fellow and then as an assistant professor at the University of Michigan in the 1960s, it was extraordinary if I had more than one African American student in my classes every couple of years. In fact, it was extraordinary if I had more than one or two women students in a class. And if I had either, they would almost certainly be among the best three or four students in the class, because only through unusual drive and commitment would these students have come to study engineering.

The change from the 1960s to 2005 at universities such as MIT and Michigan is the result of institutional leadership and occasional courage. It is the result of the determination of innumerable families and communities. And I can only conclude that despite the length of the journey, our nation is a better place than it was three decades ago because of it.

It is for this reason that I am saddened and angered by the political actions in the state of California that turned back the clock. This has been a state of great vision and action, having created the most remarkable system of public higher education in America. But today, as a direct result of Proposition 209, as well as past regental actions, only 108 of the 3,600 students in the Berkeley freshman class, or 3 percent, are known to be African Americans. My understanding is that among these freshmen the number of black students intending to study engineering is *zero*. I believe that this is a disservice to the future of California and our nation, and that it in no way represents the result of rational meritocratic selection within a color-blind society. As a pluralistic society entering a technology-dominated, highly competitive, knowledge-based age, we will need to engage the talents of all of our people, and we will need a diverse high-end workforce and leadership.

In my view, important instruments of state government and politics have collided head-on with the purposes and means of California's great universities with serious, negative consequences for our collective future. I deeply respect democracy, but I also believe that we have a responsibility to continue to make the case for race as one of many factors in university admissions, and to work toward a day when the people will return to the course from which they have dramatically veered.

THE ENDLESS FRONTIER— THE FEDERAL GOVERNMENT AND RESEARCH

In November of 1944, as the end of World War II approached, President Roosevelt wrote to Vannevar Bush, who was serving as head of the Office of Scientific Research and Development (OSRD). Roosevelt noted that the successful conclusion of the war, which he believed to be imminent, owed much to the work of U.S. scientists and engineers. He asked Bush to establish a committee to tell him how the scientific community should be organized following the war so that it could have a positive impact on the nation's economy, health, security, and quality of life in peacetime analogous to that it had had on the war effort.

Bush organized a group of committees, and in eight months delivered to President Truman his seminal and now famous report, *Science—The Endless Frontier.*[10] The fact is that Truman did not accept this report, but turned instead to William T. Golden, a bright and influential New York attorney, to produce a new study. In so doing, Golden became in essence the first presidential science advisor, and the scientific community gained a lifelong friend, supporter, and advocate. Nonetheless, the basic ideas that Bush set forth are the foundation of the most important partnership between the federal government and our universities. *Science—The Endless Frontier* also established the idea of the National Science Foundation.

By implementing the concepts of Bush's report, the United States took a radically new approach to research and development, and changed the landscape of our universities in fundamental ways. In most countries, the national infrastructure for research and development consists of public and private research laboratories that are largely disconnected from universities. The Bush report, however, proposed that U.S. public and private universities become the national R&D infrastructure. The idea was simple—the federal government would pay for the conduct of research in universities, and these research grants and contracts would enable and directly support the education of graduate students. Thus each federal dollar accomplished two objectives—generating new knowledge and technology, and simultaneously supporting the education of the next generation of scientists, engineers, and doctors.

Federal agencies, starting with the Office of Naval Research, began to implement this vision soon after the war, and in 1950 the National Science Foundation was established. Initially most funding came from the Department of Defense, and the science and engineering faculties of a handful of universities like MIT and Stanford began to build major graduate programs. More and more agencies—such as the National Institutes of Health (NIH), the Department of Energy, and later on NASA—established programs of university-based research, and the programs spread across our public and private universities and grew larger.

Major growth spurts followed externalities such as the security needs of the Cold War, our response to the Soviet launch of *Sputnik*, and the revolution in biomedical science. For example, in 1958 the Department of Defense established the Advanced Research Projects Agency (ARPA) to conceive and develop a new generation of radically different technologies to counter anticipated post-*Sputnik* threats such as Soviet intercontinental ballistic missiles and space-based weapons. ARPA funded researchers in the defense industry, private companies, and universities to conduct high-risk/high-payoff research. In the public's view, the best-known ARPA success is the Internet, most of which was developed through ARPA-sponsored research at universities. And the fourfold increase in the research budgets of the NIH that have occurred since 1970, following fundamental discoveries in cell and molecular biology and later the mapping, sequencing, and application of whole genomes, has enabled universities and academic health centers to dramatically advance basic life science and many areas of human health, and also to launch the biotechnology industry.

This federal government–university partnership has transformed our universities, has been remarkably productive, and has made us the unquestioned world leaders in research-intensive education. In the pure and elegant form of this partnership, faculty members or groups submit to federal agencies proposals to support research they believe is important. On some annual cycle these proposals are reviewed by panels of experts, and with their advice the agency selects the most intellectually meritorious ones for funding. Because research programs also require buildings, light, travel, equipment, employee benefits, and so on, the sponsoring agency supports a fair share of such *indirect costs* of research to each grant or contract.

By this ideal process, federal funds are committed through a free marketplace of ideas to support the best research done by the most talented researchers, who in turn attract the best students. Indirect costs flow together with the research, and over time a large number of excellent research-intensive universities have blossomed and huge numbers of bright young men and women have been educated and trained.

This is the golden ideal of the partnership between the federal government and our universities. It has been enormously effective and productive.

But real things do not long inhabit ideal systems. As the size and scope of the federal-university partnership have grown, so have its complexity, bureaucracy, and fiscal and political stresses. The sources of stress are well known. First and foremost, the pool of federal dollars is never sufficient to fund all the good ideas; the number of universities capable of doing very good research and advanced education has outstripped the available federal funds. Additionally, politicians are concerned that funding is not distributed appropriately across our geography. Some fields are well supported, while others are not. Many in Congress circumvent the process of merit review and simply earmark money in bills to flow to institutions or programs in their districts. Arguments about the federal government's *fair share* of indirect costs and the accounting requirements spelled out in the Office of Management and Budget's Circular A-21 are as endless as the scientific frontier envisioned by Vannevar Bush.

When our economy is threatened, as it was by the Japanese manufacturing revolution in the 1980s, many want to ignore fundamental research and emphasize R&D that can be rapidly commercialized. Some believe it is bad when large revenues flow to universities and professors based on intellectual property generated by federally sponsored research (a rare event). Agencies frequently require that institutions or companies share the costs of supporting research projects. Regulatory burdens, reporting requirements, and the number and complexity of proposals that busy faculty must write seem to expand continually. Acceptance of federal funds becomes a legal hook for the government to impose campus policies to eliminate affirmative action, to establish gender equity in athletics, or to insist on acceptance of military recruiters on campus. National-security concerns lead to arguments about what research topics should be classified and whether they should be conducted on university campuses. And since the horrific attacks on our nation on September 11, 2001, issues regarding visas for international students and scholars, their access to certain knowledge and technologies in the conduct of research and education, the control of dangerous biological agents, and the openness of scientific inquiry and communication have all become contentious issues.

So as wondrous as the federal-university partnership is, it is also a source of ongoing tensions. The sources of these tensions range from mere annoyances and political inevitabilities to matters of the deepest concern. But we must respect, nurture, and forever renew and improve this partnership.

For too long, we in universities have tended to treat our federal funding as a birthright. It is not. Leaders in Washington have very difficult jobs, and it is my experience and observation that beneath the political veneer that sometimes confounds or exasperates us, they work very hard to do what they believe is right for the country. It is our duty as faculty, students, and administrators to devote serious time and effort to better informing the public and our elected officials what we in universities do, why we do it, how we do it, and why it is crucially important to the future of the nation and world.

STATES, UNIVERSITIES, AND ECONOMIC DEVELOPMENT

During the last twenty-five years or so, there has been a dramatic increase in state-government involvement with universities, largely through R&D support aimed at enhancing the economy of the state. There is a long history of land-grant institutions supporting local economies through agricultural extension services. These federally funded entities provide support for agricultural research, but are even better known for their extension agents, who provide practical advice to farmers based on contemporary agricultural science and practice. For generations, these agencies have been valued greatly by small farm owners. But they also play a significant role in the effectiveness of schools of agriculture and agricultural engineering.

There is a parallel history of entities such as the Engineering Experiment Stations, and connections between state universities and state highway departments. The new interactions between states and universities, however, are largely aimed at the role of modern technology in the economic development of the state. Anecdotally, there would seem to be two strong waves of such state investment and engagement. The first, starting in the late

1970s and early 1980s, was aimed at improving manufacturing capabilities, thereby stimulating job growth. The motivation came when U.S. manufacturing industries found themselves to be increasingly noncompetitive in world markets as Japanese companies, especially in the automotive and consumer-electronics sectors, attained levels of quality, throughput, and efficiency that far exceeded ours. The second, more pervasive wave came about as states began to recognize that start-up companies and entrepreneurial activities had led to stunning success and job growth in some regions. It was also clear that the presence of world-class research universities was an important stimulus and participant in these economic successes. Among the primary models were Silicon Valley in California and the Route 128 corridor around Boston.

Actually, Silicon Valley and Route 128 were creations of the private sector, supported by venture capital, and not driven directly by government planning or support. They were clusters of innovation driven by a dynamic that involved both competition and cooperation among technology companies founded and supported by bright, well-educated people. However, the presence of federal laboratories, high-level defense companies, and, especially, universities whose cutting-edge research programs and education in engineering and science, all largely supported by the federal government, were essential to the phenomenon.

Route 128 had strong precursor activities starting in the 1930s, and Silicon Valley had its origins in activities of the 1950s. They were not sudden, strategically planned developments. But in the last twenty-five years, state after state, worried about stagnating industries and exported jobs, has undertaken explicit economic-development activities, frequently involving partnerships with their universities. The goal has been to revitalize old industries, jump-start new ones, and/or to attract companies headquartered elsewhere to establish factories or R&D facilities in that state.

By 1995 the fifty states collectively were investing more than $2.4 billion per year in partnerships with universities and/or industries.[11] Economic-development activities have led to direct R&D investments by state governments, 75 percent of which have gone to universities.[12] These have involved the establishment of centers of excellence in specific fields believed to have likely economic benefit in the not-too-distant future, and also activities aimed at more effectively spinning out new companies based on intellectual property developed at the universities.

I strongly believe that the role of modern research universities in economic development is critically important. I also believe that farsighted investment by states to establish research excellence and to encourage university interaction with the private sector is wise, and that state support should constitute a larger portion of the national investment in university research. However, there are several realities and pitfalls of which state government and university leaders must be cognizant.

First, these are strategic, not tactical moves. The largest return on these investments is in attracting and retaining bright, innovative people to the region and enhancing the R&D infrastructure available to them. The forces of competition, cooperation, and serendipity usually outstrip our ability to plan and predict in detail. The largest payoffs are long-term. As in the private sector, multiple seeds must be sown, and there must be a tolerance for failure. This tolerance, by the way, is one of the great differentiators between the United States and most other nations. It is essential that funds whose goal is economic development be one part of a well-balanced state budget for research universities and not serve as a substitute for core academic support. Ultimately, long-term basic research is what universities do best, and this should not be sacrificed. That said, in this age of increasingly cooperative innovation and fast-paced change, there are many opportunities to serve through "relevant" research and development that will complement, not distort, our core academic mission and bring new intellectual challenges to our faculty and students.

Second, not every state, region, or city can become the new biotech "Silicon Valley." There will only be a few such centers, and this industry may not lead to large employment. Clusters of economic development need to be based on realistic assessments and development of talent, infrastructure, and local characteristics. San Diego's emergence as a world leader in wireless communications is a great case in point. Twenty-five years ago San Diego didn't try to outperform Silicon Valley in computing, but set out on another exciting and productive path. By the way, it doesn't always have to be about the "New New Thing." It can also be about doing old things in new ways. I suspect that much of the payoff in nanotechnology will be of this nature—making everyday products with desirable new properties and characteristics.

Third, states must be careful about their assumptions regarding leveraging their funds with federal funds. Of course, a wonderful outcome of state investment in university R&D, people, and infrastructure is to slide activities ultimately onto federal support with a huge multiplier. But competition for federal funds is—or should be—strong. Not every state initiative will be leveraged and sustained in the long run by huge federal funding.

It would be especially unfortunate if the desire to leverage in this manner simply led to increased earmarking and "pork barrel" politics, thereby defeating the system of merit-based competition in a free marketplace of ideas that has made our national innovation system so effective.

Fourth, the technology-transfer activities of universities should be energetic but kept in perspective. They should have as their primary goal moving university knowledge and innovations into the private sector. It helps to recognize that the university patents that have paid enormous royalties can be counted on the fingers of one or two hands. At MIT, we are proud of our income from royalties and from small percentages of founders' stock when companies go public. But as president, I always insisted that we not build models of such income into our budgets in a way that made us dependent upon them, thereby running a risk of distorting our basic mission or bringing improper pressure on faculty members. We absolutely must maintain firm but fair policies on conflicts of interest and conflicts of commitment of time and effort.

LOCAL GOVERNMENTS—
PROGRAMS, POLITICS, AND PILOT

I once sat in a meeting listening to an excellent talk by the president of the University of Pennsylvania about the investments the university was making in programs to improve the quality of life in a long-decaying area of the city adjacent to the campus. Her leadership and perspective were interesting and meritorious. But the chancellor of an unnamed West Coast university leaned over and with good humor whispered in my ear,

"Just what am I supposed to learn from this? Our campus is surrounded by Hollywood, Westwood, and Brentwood!"

Therein lies a serious point. The community context of our campuses matters. I daresay the most complex politics most of us face are local. When as president of MIT I had to venture into meetings with officials of the City of Cambridge, I carried with me a facsimile of the letter the City Council wrote to MIT in 1916 *inviting* us to move from Boston to Cambridge. I also frequently reflected on the fact that when I came from Ann Arbor to MIT in 1990, a small reception was held to introduce me to Cambridge officials. A former mayor of the city vigorously shook my hand and said, "You must be a good guy—you are from one of only two other cities that are nuclear-free zones!" And there was the time that our athletics director was getting a haircut and started conversing with a young man, who mentioned that he was in a soccer league whose games were played on our athletics field. This was news to the director—a sort of exercise in reverse eminent domain.

Many citizens are simply antagonistic toward large institutions, and their political agendas are, to use a well-worn phrase, "up close and personal." As a consequence, the jobs of university government- and community-relations officers are second in difficulty only to those of admission and financial-aid officers.

Every university has the dilemma of wanting to be a good citizen of its town or city but knowing that its perceived deep pockets are filled with money intended for students, faculty, education, research, and campus facilities—not for other discretionary purposes. Discussions of Payments in Lieu of Taxes (PILOT) are among the most difficult we engage in. The city government often views *us* as *its* patron, but our trustees shudder to see money flowing to host cities when it is not absolutely required by law. (It is perhaps symbolic that my very last act as a university president, at 5:00 P. M. on my last day in that role at MIT, was to join the Cambridge city manager to sign a PILOT agreement.)

But I must say that, despite these inevitable tensions and frequently orthogonal views of our roles and responsibilities, some of my greatest satisfactions as president of MIT came from service-oriented programs that engaged our students, staff, and faculty as partners with other citizens of our surrounding community. Students' experiences through such activities were sometimes life changing. When I asked graduating seniors what they deeply valued in their years at MIT, the most frequent answer may well have been "tutoring kids in the Cambridge schools."

CONCLUSION

Our research-intensive public and private universities increasingly have far more similarities than differences in mission, structure, and even financial support. Our federal government, despite numerous tensions, remains our indispensable *partner*. The role of state governments toward their public universities has evolved from that of *patron* to that of *partner*—sometimes a minor partner financially. Yet at every level—federal, state, and local—governments and universities each consider themselves to be the *protagonist*, having the central role, moral authority, and last word in setting the institution's objectives and course.

Into this stew we might add philanthropists and the private sector for good measure—but despite its complexities and tensions, from it we have forged the greatest system of higher education in the world, and we must work hard and effectively to sustain and continuously improve it. We must strive for innovation and excellence, but also nurture broad access to this system and stay true to our fundamental mission of creating opportunity.

TWO

Industry, Philanthropy, and Universities

The Roles and Influences of the Private Sector in Higher Education

Today the multiversity contributes to society through a wide spectrum of activities, with academia playing the ancient and honorable roles of discoverer, conservator, interpreter, and transmitter of knowledge, values, and understanding, as well as the contemporary roles of creator of opportunity for young men and women; developer of new technologies, processes, and even products; and partner with governments, industry, and philanthropists to directly contribute to the advancement of economies, security, health, and quality of life.

As universities pursue these new roles, especially in their scientific and technological contributions to economic development, they are at the nexus of five interested parties whose expectations are frequently mutually orthogonal. *Students* are attracted to science and engineering by curiosity, awe of nature, and the excitement of the unknown. *Researchers* are driven by "fire in the belly" and obsessive concentration on solving challenging puzzles. *Legislators* at all levels believe that tax dollars should produce jobs. *Industry* wants faster and faster innovation. *Donors* want universities that implement their personal worldview.

Through an increasingly complicated, and largely implicit, integration of federal and state policies and appropriations with academic mission and means, we try to bring some coherence and synergy to these seemingly disparate aspirations. In chapter 1 I concentrated on the role of governments. My purpose here is to address the role of the private sector by exploring a few of the many interesting and continually changing interactions of universities with both industry and philanthropic individuals and organizations. I draw primarily on my personal experience, and thus claim no comprehensiveness.

INDUSTRY

U.S. corporations and corporate foundations have been a significant part of our national philanthropic community for several decades. In 2003 they made cash and in-kind donations estimated at $13.6 billion, of which 11 percent supported higher education.[1] The purposes and nature of donations to universities and other nonprofit entities have varied widely across companies and over time; however, it is fair to say that, increasingly, donations are targeted at activities and institutions that are of direct relevance to donor companies. For example, among the largest recent donations has been the approximately $40 million per year in cash and over $200 million in software that Microsoft has donated to nonprofit organizations. Such donations accomplish a lot of good and also expand potential applications and software markets in the long run. In general, the blend of philanthropic

intent, public relations, capacity building, and social agenda behind corporate giving is complex, as is the tax and regulatory
environment in which it operates. Although the distinction is
not always clear-cut, I will concentrate here on direct university-
industry interaction in research and education, rather than on
corporate philanthropy.

If one simply looks at industry as a source of support for research in U.S. universities, its role appears to be modest. In 1953
industry funded approximately 9 percent of American academic
research, and the federal government funded about 55 percent.
Then came the golden era of federal support, driven in large part
by the national reaction to the Soviet Union's launch of *Sputnik*.
Between 1960 and 1967 federal support grew to 75 percent of
the total, and industry dropped to only about 2 percent. Since
the mid-1980s industry support has been quite stable at about 8
percent of the mix, while federal support accounts for about 60
percent.[2] In other words, for decades industry has funded less
than 10 percent of university research. But this belies both the
importance and the complexity of the research relationship between academia and industry today.

The comparative advantage of the United States in world
competition is our combination of a strong R&D base and a
free-market economy. Companies and universities have critical
and intersecting roles in maintaining this advantage and building upon it. The relationship between academia and industry is
therefore of fundamental importance.

The evolving relationship between industry and academia can
be viewed in the context of the U.S. *innovation system*. This is,
effectively, a loose interaction among universities, governments,
and industry that creates new knowledge and technology through

research, educates young men and women to understand and extend it, and to move it to the marketplace in the form of goods and services. The traditional role of universities, especially their schools of science, engineering, and business, in this innovation system is relatively straightforward, but the pace of technological change, together with the forces of globalization and international competition, will almost certainly change the traditional university role substantially. We in research universities are experimenting and, at minimum, should continue to experiment carefully with new models of industry partnership and innovation. Our role in the U.S. innovation system will only increase in importance. As Alan Greenspan has stated, "In the twenty-first century, our institutions of higher learning will bear the enormous responsibility of ensuring that our society is prepared for the demands of rapid economic change."[3]

The traditional role of universities in the innovation system has its origins in Vannevar Bush's report *Science—The Endless Frontier,* to which I referred in chapter 1. This report is the basis of the unique and highly successful partnership between the federal government and our universities that has served our nation so well since the end of World War II. The model derived from this report is one in which our public and private universities are the nation's primary infrastructure for basic research. For decades, this stood in contrast to most other nations, where research was conducted primarily in independent institutes that were not affiliated with universities. Today more countries are moving toward our model. The federal government funds research in our universities, ideally selecting projects on the basis of intellectual merit to be carried out in large measure through the work of graduate students, and also contributes a *fair share* of the capital and administrative costs of doing that research. The federal dollars expended in this way do double duty: they support the quest for new knowledge and technology and simultaneously support the education of the next generation of scientists, engineers, doctors, and other researchers. The system is elegant, simple, and effective.

Although the Vannevar Bush model addresses the federal government and academia, it implies a particular two-part relationship between universities and industry to achieve the goal of using science to advance our national economy, security, health, and quality of life. First, it creates a knowledgeable workforce to work and lead in industry, bringing with it new ideas and new technological capabilities. As John Armstrong, former vice president for science and technology of IBM likes to say, "The best vehicle for technology transfer is the moving van." Second, it seems to assume that there is a linear progression from basic research to applied research to development to product and marketing, and that these components can be carried out separately in two or more organizations. It is a *laissez-faire* model, in which the commercial applications of university research are left more or less to chance: universities do the basic research, and industry may choose to commercialize it.

This approach has had phenomenal success over time. Economists broadly agree that about 50 percent of the growth of the U.S. economy during the last sixty years has been due to technical innovation, much of which has originated in university research. Universities have spawned or played the dominant role in developing such major innovations as computers, lasers, the Internet, fundamental technology for the Global Positioning Satellite (GPS) system, numerically controlled machines, the World Wide Web Consortium, financial engineering based on option pricing, the genetic revolution, and most of modern medicine.

For approximately forty-five years following the end of World War II, the American multiversity so eloquently described by Clark Kerr became the world's powerhouse for basic research in the sciences and engineering. During those same forty-five years, American industry led the world in almost every conceivable dimension, especially in mass production and in bringing new technologies to products and services. Big corporations largely dominated this era. Most developed massive central research laboratories that attracted many of the best graduates of our universities and conducted outstanding research. While emphasizing applied research of relevance to their companies, these laboratories also conducted fundamental research and contributed to the commons of scientific and technological knowledge through open publication and participation in the scientific community.

Starting in the mid-1980s two tectonic shifts occurred. First, Japanese companies began manufacturing products with levels of quality, throughput, and product cycle times that left most U.S. manufacturing companies simply unable to compete effectively in world markets. (The Japanese also became remarkable innovators, introducing world-changing products like the compact video recorder and the Sony Walkman.) Second, in the 1990s American technological entrepreneurship expanded explosively, driven mostly by advances in information technology based on microprocessors and the Internet and later by biotechnology.

America's manufacturing companies struggled to survive through painful and very basic transformations. They placed new emphasis on process management and quality control, flattened and thinned their organizations, totally reworked their product-development systems, merged research into product development in a very nonlinear manner, and eliminated the vast majority of their fundamental research and contributions to the commons of science and technology. In the end, many of these companies emerged strong and competitive. But the national innovation system had changed fundamentally. Our companies had become efficient, competitive, high-quality manufacturers, and our universities were better than ever at doing basic, or curiosity-driven, research, but many traditional linkages between companies and universities had changed.

Companies got less and less substantial innovation from their own R&D activities, which were increasingly focused on critical though incremental change. More and more, they acquired innovation by purchasing small entrepreneurial companies that had developed a product or process they needed. Universities became major players in this system, because their recent graduates and faculty formed many of those entrepreneurial companies. Frequently the university role was even more direct, enabled by the Bayh-Dole Act of 1980, which awarded to universities patent rights to inventions made in the conduct of federally sponsored research. University patent-activity and technology-transfer staffs flowered.

This period saw a number of changes and experiments in the relationship between universities and industry. First, engineering education began to change. Many of us concluded that engineering education had grown too far from its industrial roots and that we had a responsibility to our students, and within our social contract with the public, to modify our direction somewhat. Increasingly, engineering and business schools joined forces to develop both curricula and research programs in areas like modern manufacturing, product development, and entrepreneurship. A subset of faculty found intellectually challenging new problems posed by fast-paced, global, digitally connected industries.

For MIT, establishing the Leaders for Manufacturing (LFM) program ushered in this period of change. LFM was established in 1988 as an educational and research partnership among industry, the School of Engineering, and the Sloan School of Management, with one co-director from each. Initially it had eleven corporate partners from several different manufacturing sectors—such as aerospace, automotive, electronics, and medical products—each of which provided several million dollars of financial support and also committed high-level professional effort to joint projects. Our experience with this program taught us several important lessons, among them that when companies provide large financial support, they establish effective access and working relationships with their leaders and best thinkers; that interdisciplinary and inter-school programs can be successful; that knowledge transfer from academia to industry can be accelerated; and that academicians can contribute directly and effectively to solving stimulating, challenging, and important problems posed by today's industry.

Corporate/University Research Partnerships

During the 1990s, MIT established a small number of partnerships with individual companies, each in a different industrial sector. The intent of these partnerships was to undertake challenging research in areas of mutual strategic interest to MIT faculty and to the company. Each partnership was supported at a level of roughly $5 million per year, with an intended life of at least five years. They were intended to fill a void in U.S. research created by the demise or transformation of so many corporate research laboratories, to stimulate change and renewal in engineering and management education, and to diversify our portfolio of research support, which in my view had become overly dependent on federal funding.

Most of these partnerships were established by a commitment at the corporate level, usually by the CEO, that such a partnership would be funded if the faculty from the university, together with technology and thought leaders in the company, successfully defined an important research program that clearly added value to both organizations. Thus there was a *potential* top-down commitment, but—and I must strongly emphasize this—it would come to fruition only through bottom-up faculty and company interest and commitment. That is a *sine qua non*.

These partnerships were established in areas such as the environment, biotechnology, advanced information technology, financial engineering, and biologically based materials. Partner companies included Amgen, Merck, Ford, NTT, Merrill Lynch, DuPont, Microsoft, and Hewlett-Packard. Over time, several interesting characteristics evolved. All of these partnerships engaged multiple academic departments, and indeed multiple schools, and all ended up with significant educational objectives—development of new courses and pedagogy, as well as student support. Another characteristic was summarized by an outstanding biology professor, who wrote, "Without this industry support, my lab would be doing nothing really new, because our federal support has become so risk averse." Those partnerships that worked really well did so when a high level of trust and mutual respect developed between the university and industry participants, and when there was a clear understanding of the differing goals and time frames of the two organizations.

At the same time, such major industry support was viewed by most faculty participants as requiring high maintenance. Renewal of partnerships for additional years was to some extent captive to the ups and downs of the company's economic fortunes. Sometimes the quality or longevity of the partnerships diminished when company leadership changed. Nonetheless several partnerships, though not all, were mutually judged to be very successful and have been extended well beyond the initial commitment.

A common concern is whether such major interactions and support distort the mission of the university. Good people may well disagree on this. My own view is that they expand the intellectual opportunity space in which some faculty and students engage in a very positive way, and that faculty will not permit anything they consider to be distortion. A faculty-wide survey and study of the partnerships was conducted in 2002, and it concluded that while many faculty members worried that such distortion might occur, no one could site an instance in which they believed it actually had.

Finally, what about intellectual property? This was a major issue in negotiating agreements, but MIT's industry partnerships are conducted within our normal policies on intellectual property, which are based on university ownership of intellectual property in the first instance and open publication of research results.

Intellectual Property

Universities hold dear their role in discovering and disseminating knowledge. The underlying assumption is that what we do on our campuses is, or should be, of general value to society and should be shared openly as a social good. There can be a tension between the policy of open sharing and the fact that much of the knowledge we generate, especially in science and engineering, has economic value—that is, it is intellectual property to which the inventor and the institution have legitimate claim. Unfortunately, in my view, some universities maintain unrealistic expectations about striking it rich through patent royalties and have tended to be overly protective and difficult when it comes to negotiating sponsored research agreements. But on the whole, the sensible management of intellectual property is a plus in university interaction with society.

Companies, on the other hand, must compete to create value for their customers and financial gain for their stockholders. Therefore they have an interest in holding closely the knowledge and the techniques that give them a competitive advantage. Patent ownership is a tool both for protection of their competitive advantage and for maximizing profits, by charging for their use and by avoiding paying royalties to others, including universities. The time from fundamental discovery to commercialization has decreased dramatically in many fields, and margins of competitive advantage have become very small and fleeting in many fast-paced industries.

Views about university intellectual property seem to vary, largely based on the maturity and scale of the industry in question. It is also generally the case that industry leaders at the highest ranks within corporations seem to be much more flexible on intellectual-property issues than those making operational, project-level decisions.

Universities' approaches to patents should be designed primarily to encourage the transfer of technology to the private sector. This requires an ability to negotiate with industrial sponsors as equals, which is best accomplished, in my view, by university ownership of intellectual properties produced by campus researchers, coupled with flexibility in reaching agreements with sponsors about licenses. When projects are large, such as the strategic partnerships I discussed above, the negotiation process seems to work well. However, I believe academia would be well served to establish a voluntary, nationwide standard agreement for more routine industry-sponsored research projects. The Government-University-Industry Research Roundtable (GUIRR) convened by the National Academies has championed such an approach.[4]

Knowledge Integration Communities

A quite different model for industry/university interaction is developing within the Cambridge-MIT Institute (CMI). CMI is an alliance of Cambridge University and MIT, funded primarily by the U.K. government, initially for six years. Industry also supports CMI through sponsorship of specific research projects. The mission of CMI is to enhance the competitiveness, productivity, and entrepreneurship of the United Kingdom by improving the effectiveness of knowledge exchange between universities and industry; educating leaders; creating new ideas; developing programs for change in universities, industry, and government; and building networks of participants beyond the two universities.

The formation of Knowledge Integration Communities (KICs) for CMI research projects is an attempt to enhance feedback and efficiency through knowledge exchange, and to do so in a manner that elicits enthusiasm among the academic researchers who do the creative work. In other words, CMI research is intended to generate fundamental new ideas that are developed with some explicit consideration of potential use and an eye toward the needs of industry. The stakeholders who comprise a KIC typically include academic researchers, industry participants from large and small companies, government policy makers, special-interest groups such as regional development authorities, and educators from a variety of institutions, who come together to pursue a common science, technology, and social end goal. Although this broad involvement runs counter to many academic instincts, it appears to be working rather well because considerable thought and effort have been put into the process and because the concept itself arose out of careful discussion and iterative planning among the stakeholders. I believe the KICs' initial success also reflects the fact that the topics of the research, such as silent aircraft, quantum computing, and next-generation drug discovery, are truly exciting and challenging.

CMI's KICs are works in progress. More years of experience will be required to rigorously evaluate their effectiveness. Indeed, the hope and intent is for the KICs to develop into long-term, self-sustaining activities. Louis Pasteur famously observed, "Chance favors the well-prepared mind." I consider that the goal of the KICs is to support excellent fundamental research, but to create a *collective prepared mind* of multiple stakeholders that enhances the probability that results will find positive industrial application. This is a way of operating in what Donald Stokes dubbed "Pasteur's Quadrant,"[5] with research projects seeking fundamental understanding but being inspired by potential utility.

Despite my enthusiasm for meeting academia's responsibilities as part of our national innovation system, I also believe that we must take great care as we develop new relations with industry so that universities do not assume a posture that is overly utilitarian. In time this would erode universities' intellectual independence and their ability to serve as objective critics of society. Indeed, there is a paradox in that it is this very independence and objectivity that usually attracts industry to work jointly with academia. The right balance must be struck. As we work together in areas that have policy implications, such as the environment, energy, telecommunications, and productivity, we must maintain our independence and objectivity. Thus it is in the best interests of both parties that these matters be addressed carefully and resolved.

PHILANTHROPY

Milton Eisenhower, president of the Johns Hopkins University from 1956 to 1967, is said to have had a very concise fund-raising speech: "Higher education and business are basically interdependent. One needs money to produce educated people, and the other needs educated people to produce money."[6] Needless to say, today our society, universities, and philanthropy—and our fund-raising speeches—are not so simple! But the fundamental implication that higher education prepares men and women to advance society, and that this worthy activity costs money, certainly is true today.

The Growing Importance of Gifts and Endowments

In an ideal world, one might imagine, private colleges and universities would derive all of their revenue from two sources—tuition income and gifts plus the annual return from a sizable endowment—and public institutions would derive all of their revenue from tuition income and state appropriations. But today this is a pipe dream. Both public and private colleges and universities now require that significant fractions of their support come from individuals and private organizations, including gifts and income from endowment. For example, consider the sixty-two leading research universities belonging to the Association of American Universities (AAU). According to a recent study, the distribution of annual *expenditures* of the public and private AAU universities are remarkably similar: 34 percent for instruction and 23 percent for research in the privates; and 32 percent for instruction and 25 percent for research in the publics.[7]

But what are the sources of *revenue* for these activities? Twenty-two percent of the annual revenues of the *private* AAU universities, excluding their hospitals, comes from private gifts, grants, and contracts; 20 percent comes from tuition, net of financial aid; and 25 percent comes from federal, state, and local government grants and contracts. (The remaining 33 percent comes from auxiliary enterprises, sales, services, and miscellaneous sources.) Of the equivalent annual revenues of the *public* AAU universities, excluding their hospitals, 9 percent comes from private gifts, grants, and contracts; 13 percent comes from tuition, net of financial aid; and 31 percent comes from federal, state, and local government funds. As indicated by these statistics, and as discussed in some depth in chapter 1, many leading public universities are rapidly becoming very dependent on private-sector support—indeed, elements of several of these universities are actually or effectively privatized. The continued excellence of both our public and our private universities—and access to them by students of modest financial means—will be increasingly dependent on private philanthropy.

Thus a fundamental question is whether many state universities will be able to establish endowments equal to the task. In 2005 only $84 billion, or 28 percent, of endowment holdings were in public universities, while the privates held $215 billion, or 72 percent.[8] Yet because the public institutions enroll a vastly greater number of students than the privates, the asymmetry is much greater than these numbers imply: among the 746 colleges and universities in the 2005 National Association of College and University Business Officers (NACUBO) Endowment Study, the average endowment per student was $17,195 in the public institutions and $111,629 in the privates. Nonetheless, there are suggestions that the likely answer is yes, over time a number of state universities could build substantial endowments. A recent analysis of college and university endowments exceeding $200 million indicates that the endowments of public institutions are growing at a faster rate than the endowments of the private schools.[9] Why?

Consider the apocryphal story about an American tourist who visited one of the ancient colleges of Oxford and admired its beautiful and perfect lawns. He asked a groundskeeper to tell him the secret of developing such a perfect lawn. The groundskeeper thought for a few minutes and replied, "Well, it's simple. You just water it, weed it, and roll it . . . for about eight hundred years."

We tend to think of university endowments in the same way, that to be large they must be very old and that they grow primarily by effective investment and spending policies. While this is true to an extent, the fact is that university endowments grow almost as much by the annual addition of gifts as they do through investment, and it appears that the publics are adding gifts at a relatively faster rate than the privates. Of the colleges and universities included in the NACUBO study cited above, the public institutions added an average of about 5 percent of their endowments' market values each year between 1999 and 2004, while the privates added about 2 percent per year.

One can speculate on the reasons for this, including the scale of the donor base relative to endowment size, differences in how capital projects are funded, and so on, but there are two clear messages: first, annual fund-raising is very important, and second, in a few decades we can anticipate some well-endowed public institutions if they set that as part of their strategy.

A Dynamic and Challenging Environment for Fund-Raising

During the last two decades in this country, we have developed a knowledge-based economy. Increasingly, innovation and entrepreneurial activity have stimulated the growth of both employment and equities, and we have simultaneously leveled or reduced tax rates and frequently reduced public services with the purpose of driving economic growth. Associated with this growth is an implied responsibility of the business sector and of individuals whose wealth has grown dramatically to voluntarily bear more of the costs of critical social goods—including, in my view, education.

Is this happening? Does private support have the requisite staying power for colleges and universities, whose capabilities and excellence must be sustained for a very long time? Is there an unacceptable volatility in philanthropic support? And will there be an appropriate long-term match of donors' values and goals with the values, goals, and core needs of the academy?

We are at least off to a good start. Philanthropic support of higher education in America is continuing to grow. Between 1994 and 2004 annual voluntary support of higher education grew by 94 percent in constant dollars, and even when normalized to the growing number of enrolled students, it still grew by 84 percent.[10] Throughout this period, about half of the giving was by individuals, roughly equally divided between alumni and non-alumni. The other half of the gifts came from corporations, foundations, and religious and other organizations.

Not surprisingly, annual gift support has some identifiable relation to the state of the economy. Indeed, it is rather strongly correlated with the New York Stock Exchange Index.[11] This level of volatility in giving should be acceptable, and to the extent that gifts are placed in endowment, or at least treated as endowment, such fluctuations are smoothed. As noted in chapter 1, however, during the dot-com era fluctuations were so strong that they did have important effects in the operating budgets of most private universities. But in general the private support of most schools grows slowly and steadily.

It also is a fact of life that the ability of private universities to maintain their excellence, and of public universities to continue to build their endowments and gift streams, will depend in very large measure on the philanthropic priorities set by the coming generation of the wealthiest Americans. To see why this is so, note that in a typical capital campaign for a large university, approximately 80 percent of the total comes from gifts of $1 million or more. This signals that the views of the very wealthiest donors and foundations are critically important bellwethers. Their large gifts often have important directional or even transformational significance.

There is one trend in this important community of extremely generous donors that I find particularly significant—the changing balance between their giving to K–12 and to higher education. The new generation of education philanthropists, whose wealth mostly has come from successful entrepreneurship, has turned much of its attention to the daunting problem of improving K–12 education in this nation. For many decades, we in America have lived with the strange situation of having the finest system of higher education in the world while our system of public primary and secondary education fails in many important dimensions. The national ramifications of problems in the K–12 system are accelerating rapidly because many of our young people are not prepared to succeed in a rapidly globalizing economy and highly competitive international marketplace.

According to a recent article in the *New York Times*, in 1990 grants to higher education of $10,000 or more from 1,010 of the larger foundations totaled about $500 million, while those to K–12 totaled about $200 million.[12] In 2003 grants to higher education totaled approximately $1.12 billion, but the K–12 grants had grown to $1.23 billion. As one who believes deeply in the centrality of education at all levels to our national well-being, I do not view this philanthropic trend toward primary and secondary education as negative in any way. But it is a stark reminder that it will be no easy feat to continually increase the dependence of both public and private universities and colleges on charitable giving to provide their margins of excellence, innovation, and access.

In the domain of individual philanthropy, there are many other changes and challenges ahead as well. For example, in today's competitive environment it is increasingly important to provide fellowships to graduate students. Even in the sciences and engineering, where graduate students generally are supported as research assistants paid by research grants and contracts, philanthropically supported fellowships, especially for the first year of study, are now very important competitive tools. In my experience, this need is generally not well understood by the graduates of our universities who are potential donors, because most of those who now are able to provide such funds graduated in the 1960s and 1970s, when federal research support was quite readily available, both through research assistantships and also through massive federal-agency-based fellowships, such as those established under the National Defense Education Act (NDEA). This is a prime example of the complexity of matching donor passions and objectives with core institutional needs.

Face it, the grand challenge of university fund-raising is just that—matching donor passions and objectives with core institutional needs and faculty aspirations and priorities. The art form of accomplishing this is even more difficult today, when donors are increasingly businesslike about their gifts and, quite understandably, especially sensitive to results, metrics, milestones, and so on. This is exacerbated by the fact that today universities also bring enormous bureaucratic detail and complexity to major gift negotiations and agreements, because we must operate under ever-expanding federal regulations and the requirements of oversight groups like the Financial Accounting Standards Board (FASB). Even regulations and controls imposed by state governments and attorneys general increasingly come into play. In the environment created by the Sarbanes-Oxley Act governing corporate accounting and board responsibilities, trustees and regents also have become more concerned about detailed language and controls regarding private gifts.

And the word that strikes the most terror in the hearts of academic fund-raisers and administrators is *leverage*. Today's prototypical donor expects that his or her gift, particularly when it is associated with research, should be matched by the institution, by other donors, or by federal research grants. Private foundations that support research recoil at the prospect of paying the full indirect costs associated with that research, so those costs must be paid by the institution from other resources. (It is hard for many to accept that universities have a legal obligation to fund such indirect costs because federal regulations forbid charging any research sponsor a lower indirect cost rate than that charged to government grants and contracts.)

Such issues become particularly complicated when large research laboratories, centers, or institutes are established based on private donations. This requires careful balancing of the interests and fiscal realities of all four parties I mentioned at the beginning of this lecture—students, researchers, donors, and government and industry actors. Because such organizations frequently have some degree of autonomy and desire to be free of what both donors and researchers consider to be university bureaucracy, complicated governance issues arise as well. But we simply have to devote the necessary time, thought, and energy to resolving these matters, because the rewards are great. Done right, such laboratories, centers, and institutes are among the strongest means by which modern universities can contribute to the long-term welfare of society. Done wrong, they can fail because they are not well integrated into the deepest intellectual life of the university, are built on unsustainable financial models, or are insufficiently flexible over time.

Other trends also raise questions about the future of private philanthropy to colleges and universities. What will be the effect of changing demographics, especially the large number of graduate students who now come from other countries and other societies? I can think of many remarkably generous gifts to U.S. universities from international alumni who became successful U.S. entrepreneurs, or who returned home but wanted others from their part of the world to gain an American education. But I worry that the perceived and/or real diminishing openness and welcoming attitude of our country in the post-9/11 era may have major ramifications regarding international philanthropy in the years ahead. Hopefully this will play out in a more positive manner, but that remains to be seen.

More broadly, globalization raises multiple questions about the future of philanthropic support for U.S. universities. Major American donors, companies, and foundations are increasingly turning their attention to health and other issues in the developing world. I strongly salute this, but it could have ramifications for U.S. academia. International donors who in the past have supported the excellence of U.S. universities may believe it is now time to turn their attention to growing the higher-educational capacity within their own countries. I salute this, too, and hope that the emerging meta-university I discuss in chapter 4 will allow us to encourage and enable such capacity building. But again, it could impact future gifts to our institutions.

At the corporate and governmental level, some nations, especially Japan, have passed through various stages in their development of industrial and economic power. In the 1980s and 1990s many Japanese companies made generous investments in certain U.S. universities. For example, MIT today has more than thirty professorships endowed by Japanese companies. These, in my view, were wise investments. They were very helpful to us in building our excellence in a wide variety of fields and also established mutually beneficial personal and professional relationships between some of our best professors and Japanese companies and leaders. It also provided opportunities for our faculty and students to know and appreciate another country and culture and to form more global perspectives. This helped many of our students become more valuable employees of U.S. companies as globalization proceeded. Frankly, it also provided first-rate academic advice and interactions for Japanese companies during the waning years of an academic culture and, indeed, of legal restrictions in Japan that did not encourage their own universities to work with industry.

Finally, and most obviously, many global companies based in the United States are now investing substantially in other countries by establishing R&D facilities and also by expanding technology and management education there. It is in these companies' best interests to build technical capacity, human capital, and expanded future consumer bases in countries moving up the economic ladder. Clearly, it also is very cost effective, given the dramatically lower wage scales in many other countries. Again,

I strongly believe that expanding education and knowledge generation worldwide is among the very worthiest of goals, but we cannot be oblivious to its effects here at home.

Student Financial Aid

To complete this discussion of higher-education philanthropy, let me comment in some detail about the structure, trends, and issues of student financial aid. Financial aid is arguably the most important and, traditionally, a highly popular and prevalent use of private gifts in both public and private universities.

All institutions of higher learning in the United States strive for *excellence* and *access* of students to that excellence. In all but a few of the wealthiest schools, these goals clash when an institution decides the purpose of its financial aid. The amount of financial aid available and the philosophy that governs its use are major determinants of who attends the school, for the simple reason that they are key to establishing the actual price of attendance that must be borne by a student and his or her family.

Financial aid is also an area in which both partnership and conflicts between the federal government and colleges—and between colleges and parents—are common. It is a matter that evokes emotion, politics, conflicting philosophies, and misunderstanding. My purpose for exploring aspects of these issues here is that private giving is key to financial aid in most institutions, and it is an area where the sands are shifting rapidly.

Gordon Winston points out with great clarity that colleges are strange businesses.[13] In traditional businesses, a company produces a product. There is a *cost* incurred to produce the product. The product is offered to potential customers for a *price*. If customers are willing to pay a price that exceeds the cost, the company can make a profit and continue in business. If the market can only sustain a price that is less than the cost of producing the product, the company fails and goes out of that business.

Colleges and universities, however, provide a service that almost always costs more than many students can or will pay. In business terms, they operate at a loss that must be made up by a *subsidy*. In a public university, much of that subsidy is provided by state appropriations. In private institutions, much of the subsidy is provided by funds and endowments largely built from gifts and bequests from alumni and other private donors.

An important component of the subsidy is financial aid—that is, grants and loans to students and their families. In both public and private colleges and universities, the federal government provides some financial aid to many students. The relative amount and nature of the financial aid provided by the federal government versus that provided by institutions has changed dramatically during the last few decades.

In 1971 about 50 percent of the financial aid provided to post-secondary students was in the form of direct grants, that is, *scholarships* from the federal government; about 20 percent was *grants* from the institutions (primarily derived from individual philanthropic giving); and approximately 30 percent was in the form of *loans* from the federal government. Thus 80 percent of the financial aid came from the government, predominantly in the form of direct grants.

For a brief period in the late 1970s, federal grants soared to about 70 percent of the mix and federal loans were about 20 percent. By 1990 federal grants had dropped dramatically, to only 15 percent of the total financial aid; 25 percent was grants provided by the institutions; and nearly 60 percent was in the form of federal loans—a mix that has been fairly stable for over a decade. Thus today almost 80 percent of the financial aid still comes from the federal government, and it is predominantly in the form of loans; only 24 percent of the federal aid to students is in the form of direct grants. It should be noted, however, that the loan-to-grant ratio is much higher for the graduate-student population than for undergraduates.

In constant dollars—that is, purchasing power—total federal expenditures on student grants grew by 96 percent between 1971 and 2004, whereas grants made by institutions using private funds grew by 600 percent and federal loans to students grew by 830 percent. This enormous growth of federal loans relative to federal grants is a major factor in the economics of American higher education.[14]

During the last two decades, the purpose of institutional financial aid, which, as we have seen, now comprises about half of the total grant (scholarship) funds provided to students, has been vigorously debated in the academic community. Basically, grants are given either as need-based aid or as merit-based aid, and this is at the core of the clash between the values of excellence and access.

Need-based financial aid is distributed to students in proportion to a measure of the student's and his or her family's ability to pay the tuition, fees, and room-and-board charges necessary to attend a college to which he or she has been admitted. An institution that is fully committed to need-based financial aid considers that all of the students it admits are academically meritorious, and our covenant with them is that if they are admitted, we will make sure that they can attend, regardless of their financial capability. Need is assessed on a case-by-case basis by using standard federal forms, sometimes supplemented with additional information, to determine the amount a family is reasonably able to pay for the student's education. The difference between that amount and the sum of tuition, room and board, and other expenses is provided to the student as some combination of institutional and federal grants and loans. Some obligation to work to earn a fraction of the cost is also included. Thus in an institution dedicated to need-based aid, a student from a poor family will pay very little, while a student from a very wealthy family will pay most or all of the cost of attendance.

Merit-based financial aid is distributed to students in recognition of high academic merit—that is, demonstrated intellectual excellence—or, in some cases, artistic or athletic excellence. The amount of the institutional grant to a student in this case is independent of the student's or family's wealth. Thus it is equally likely, or arguably more likely, to go to a student who could reasonably afford to pay a substantial portion of the cost of attendance.

An institution that awards most or all of its financial aid on the basis of merit generally sees it as a means to compete against other schools for excellent students who will increase the academic quality of the institution. Many such universities administer financial aid through the practice of *enrollment management*—that is, they deploy these and other resources in a way designed to maximize the quality of their student body. A school that awards grants predominantly or entirely on the basis of need generally views financial aid as a charitable resource to provide access for talented students to an expensive education that they otherwise could not afford. It is in this sense that the values of excellence and access come into conflict.

A court case involving MIT has particular relevance to this conflict and to the current state of need-based financial aid, especially in private institutions. Let me digress briefly to review it.

The Overlap Lawsuit

In May 1991 U.S. attorney general Richard Thornburgh brought a formal complaint against the eight Ivy League universities and MIT, charging that they had illegally colluded in the Overlap Group, a set of colleges and universities that held meetings to assure that financial aid to students applying to more than one of these institutions was awarded only on the basis of financial need.[15] The next week he left the administration to run for the U.S. Senate. This was a bizarre application of the Sherman Anti-Trust Act; indeed, it was the first time that a nonprofit organization had been sued under this act. That fact undoubtedly brought a lot of zealousness to Justice Department attorneys who sensed a new legal frontier to pursue.

The Justice Department claimed that the institutions were conspiring to set financial-aid levels in a noncompetitive way, but what really was at stake was the future of the view that the role of financial aid is to enable those who would not otherwise be able to attend a fine university to do so. The other eight institutions signed a consent decree, essentially a way of saying that they had done nothing wrong but wouldn't do it again. MIT decided to challenge the Justice Department in court.

MIT had long believed and believes today that undergraduate financial aid exists to enable bright students who come from families of modest means to attend college. We admit students on the basis of their merit, and we distribute financial aid on the basis of their need. For many years prior to 1991, the eight Ivy League schools, MIT, and about forty other institutions had been mutually committed to these principles. Every year we compared data on the financial need of those students who had been admitted to more than one of our institutions. Using a common methodology, we compared the judgments of our financial-aid officers on each of these families' ability to pay a share of the cost of their child's education. We made no common decisions about what tuition to charge or how much aid to provide, but we did make a common assessment of their need.

What then happened? There was a protracted and dramatic legal battle. Economic experts argued, newspapers editorialized in our favor, and eloquent witnesses testified about the virtues of MIT's system of merit-based admission and need-based financial aid. We predicted that if we did not prevail, the nation's financial-aid system would spin apart and more and more financial aid would become merit-based—that is, be given to very good students who did not actually need it in order to recruit them to campuses.

MIT lost the case in the U.S. Circuit Court in Philadelphia. Within hours, to the utter astonishment of the Justice Department, I held a press conference and announced that we would appeal the ruling. The three-judge appellate court heard our arguments, and ruled on September 17, 1993. There were three legal points in question. The court ruled unanimously in favor of MIT on two points and split two to one in MIT's favor on the third point. It remanded the case back to the lower court. For all intents and purposes, we had won a strong victory. On this basis, we negotiated a settlement with the Justice Department that defined terms under which limited agreements and after-the-fact data comparisons could be made by colleges. These ground rules were further expanded and refined in subsequent reauthorizations of the federal Higher Education Act.

The appeal hearing, normally a very brief and dry affair, had some real drama. We were pleased to accept the enthusiastic offer of the distinguished jurist Leon Higgenbotham to present supporting amicus briefs to the court. He had served as chief justice of that very court until only a few weeks before the hearing. I recall attending a Martin Luther King Day speech he presented at MIT in 1995 and hearing him state that the two pro bono legal endeavors he was most proud of in his career were representing Nelson Mandela and testifying on behalf of MIT. Why? Because he deeply believed that the decades of commitment by the Overlap schools to merit-based admission and need-based financial aid had been a fair and powerful tool in advancing talented underrepresented minorities in American society.

Nonetheless, the Ivies remained under the consent decree for a decade, and the use of merit aid grew across the country. Many colleges and universities now bargain with parents, matching offers of other schools and trying to maximize the number of top students they can attract with a given financial-aid budget. An entire cottage industry of advisors has grown up to assist families in the wheeling and dealing. Clearly, the institutional aid resources of private colleges and universities are increasingly consumed in bidding wars for affluent students, absorbing revenues that could be used instead to offer better aid packages to high-need students and/or to offer admission and aid to larger numbers of high-need students.[16]

In 2000 a group of twenty-eight leading universities and colleges, including Cornell, Stanford, Yale, and MIT, signed a public document committing themselves to merit-based admission and to a common methodology for measuring need.[17] This was an attempt to nudge the system back in the general direction of its pre-1991 configuration. It is helpful, but the merit-aid approach is strong in many other universities.

Despite this imperfect ending, I still believe that this was a legal battle worth fighting, and we resisted unwarranted government intrusion into the business of private universities. To be sure, this was victory in a battle, not in the war. We must continue to be on guard against the perennial attempts to increase federal control of academic affairs.

At the current time, discussions about cost, price, subsidy, and the roles of both governments and institutions in the economics of higher education are most frequently conducted in the context of cost, benefit, and competition, viewing the individual student as a price-conscious consumer/customer. This is understandable, especially given the all-too-real middle-class squeeze. But I believe that there are larger issues of policy and the social contract among universities, governments, and society, and that all three sectors must struggle with achieving the proper balance. It is clear to me that we are far from finding the right balance of financial aid and educational price needed for many young people to fulfill the American dream. Seventy-eight percent of high-school graduates who score in the top quartile on standardized tests but come from families in the lowest income quartile attend college. However, the identical percentage of high-school graduates who score poorly on the same standardized tests but come from families in the highest income quartile attend college.[18]

The federal Pell Grant program, which is aggressively targeted at helping low-income students, dominates federal grant aid to undergraduate students. But today the federal government spends as much on income-tax credits and deductions for educational expenses as it does on Pell Grants. This helps to attenuate the middle-class squeeze, but, like some merit aid, tax credits and deductions also subsidize even the wealthiest students.

In many states, as with the Queen in *Alice in Wonderland,* there is a sense of having to run harder and harder just to stay in the same place, because tuitions have risen rapidly because state appropriations have stagnated. Despite the rapid increases (in percentage terms), tuition at state universities and colleges is still reasonably affordable for middle-income students, but frequently state aid resources have not increased fast enough to prevent these tuition rises from imposing growing burdens on low-income students attending public institutions. This is exacerbated by the fact that many states and state institutions are devoting an increasing fraction of their grant aid to merit-based scholarships.

From all of this, I conclude that funds and endowments for student grants—particularly scholarships for undergraduates— will only be more important in the future. Having engaged in university fund-raising since the 1980s, I have observed that supporting financial aid is very popular among alumni. Innumerable times I have heard graduates say, "I could never have attended MIT if it were not for financial aid, and I want the next generation of students to have the same opportunity." This is one of the reasons that I believe so passionately in maximizing institutional commitment to need-based aid. It will be critically important to maintain and enhance the spirit of private generosity toward student support in the changing and increasingly complex context described here.

CONCLUSION

In public as well as private universities, resources provided by philanthropic individuals and foundations and by corporate research sponsors increasingly support the margin of university excellence, as well as the access of students to that excellence. The endowments of public universities are growing faster than those of private colleges and universities. Universities and industry should increasingly work together as components of our national innovation system—a system that is challenged by globalization and accelerating rates of technological change. The congruence of interests, goals, and expectations of philanthropists and corporate sponsors with those of universities must be carefully considered. The values of excellence and access frequently come into conflict as schools decide how to award student financial aid from gifts and endowments on the basis of merit or on the basis of financial need. Despite such interesting and important challenges, the generosity of individuals and foundations and the support of farsighted corporations and industry consortia are central to maintaining and enhancing America's outstanding system of higher education.

THREE

Openness

*Education, Research, and
Scholarly Communication in an
Age of Globalization and Terrorism*

Of all the things that have changed since Clark Kerr's 1963 God-kin Lectures, I suspect that the extent of the internationalization of our faculties and graduate-student populations in science, engineering, and management is one of the most dramatic. This change is matched or exceeded by the role of new communications and information technologies that connect and inform us instantaneously throughout our campuses and around the globe. These are two important aspects of the essential openness of American universities.

I have come to believe that the openness of American campuses in many dimensions is one of our most important defining characteristics. Openness describes the state of our research universities at the beginning of the twenty-first century, and it establishes a remarkable field of opportunity and responsibility in the globalization of higher education going forward. But today our openness is also threatened, largely because of our national struggle to come to grips with the reality of terrorism.

My purpose here is to share some thoughts about the inter-connection of such seemingly disparate themes as the Age of the Internet, terrorism, and the global opportunity and responsibility of universities.

THINGS WE TAKE FOR GRANTED

Faculty and students of my generation, and certainly those who are younger, take for granted the open flow across the borders of our campuses and nation—the open flow of students, scholars, faculty, scientific and scholarly information, and educational knowledge and tools.

Our nearly unanimous opinion undoubtedly is that the openness of our national borders and especially of our campuses to talented men and women from other lands is a major factor in our academic excellence, our cultural richness, our economic success, and, in a strategic sense, our national security. At MIT, we are very proud of the Nobel Laureates who teach and work on our campus. Those who received their Nobel Prizes in recent decades were born in the United States, India, Germany, Italy, Mexico, and Japan. Similarly, the recent Laureates from the University of California were born in the United States, Taiwan, Poland, France, Hungary, Germany, Austria, and Norway.

In a similar manner, universities like the University of California and MIT have prided themselves in being meritocracies that benefit from, and provide opportunity to, talented students from across America's broad spectrum of cultural, economic, and racial backgrounds. As a private institution, MIT would add geographic background to this list, and so would the University of California, though within the constraints of an institution designed to serve California citizens first and foremost.

We also would take as a given that scientific and scholarly knowledge should freely pass back and forth across our campus boundaries. Science thrives in unfettered communication among scientists everywhere, and has always had an international culture. Indeed, the conduct of science requires criticism and testing of the repeatability of experiments by other scientists. Scholarly pursuits more broadly require access to knowledge and artifacts, and are strengthened by criticism and exploration from different vantage points. One need only look back to the history of the Soviet Union to understand that science, even that practiced by brilliant and well-educated scholars, cannot flourish in isolation.

Historically, the openness of scientific and technological knowledge has been challenged in two ways: by issues of classification or voluntary withholding of knowledge that may endanger national or international security; and by concerns that arise regarding potentially valuable intellectual property and proprietary knowledge when university researchers interact with the private sector. But for the most part, great universities come down on the side of the open flow of knowledge within their campuses and to and from the world beyond. Sometimes, in what we deem to be the national interest, we conduct classified work in special, segregated units, like the University of California's Department of Energy laboratories and MIT's Lincoln Laboratory, which is operated primarily for the Department of Defense. Of course, we generally have strong rules to ensure the open publication of the results of our campus research, and we demand that all students have access to all campus research.

Finally, we certainly assume that our courses are open to all qualified and appropriately registered students. Furthermore, through textbook publication and various electronic means, we frequently share the formal content of our classes with others.

OPENNESS: THE POST-9/11 WORLD

We are all painfully aware that in September 2001 international terrorism arrived on our shores with the horrific attacks on the World Trade Center and the Pentagon, and the contemporaneous tragedy in the fields of rural Pennsylvania.

To establish context, let me turn back the clock to February 15, 2001, when the U.S. Commission on National Security/21st Century, co-chaired by former senators Gary Hart and Warren Rudman, released a report. In chillingly prescient language, the Hart-Rudman Commission stated: "The combination of unconventional weapons proliferation with the persistence of international terrorism will end the relative invulnerability of the U.S. homeland to catastrophic attack. A direct attack against American citizens on American soil is likely over the next quarter century."[1]

The U.S. scientific and educational communities are aware that in this report the Commission also stated: "Second only to a weapon of mass destruction detonating in an American city, we can think of nothing more dangerous than a failure to manage properly science, technology, and education for the common good over the next quarter century."[2]

The interplay between the issue of terrorism and the "management of science, technology, and education for the common good" became all too real in the fall of 2001. Just three weeks after the attacks on New York and Washington, I participated in a previously scheduled seminar on science policy together with other academicians, technologists, and a bipartisan group of current and former senators and congressmen. Before we began our meeting, the chair went around the table and asked each of us to share a few immediate thoughts regarding the terrorist attacks. In his characteristically concise and insightful manner, former defense secretary and Stanford professor William Perry responded that he had two things to say: first, that there would be a very forceful military response, and second, that guarding our civil liberties would need to be a strong priority in the months ahead. And this is precisely how things have played out.

The federal government thus had thrust upon it a daunting responsibility to protect the lives of people in the United States—but to do so within a new, complicated environment far different than that of the Cold War years, during which much of our national-security policy had been shaped. Protecting citizens is, of course, a fundamental responsibility of our government. Productive consideration of the ramifications of terrorism defense for our universities, or the conduct of effective dialog with federal officials, must begin with the recognition of this responsibility.

This new world of homeland and international security also presented opportunities to the research-university community to serve the nation through security-related R&D. MIT is engaged in such service in a variety of ways, as is the University of California. But the academic community also recognized very quickly that reactions to these all-too-real dangers would inevitably pose conflicts with some of our most deeply held values, and indeed with the fundamental methodology of science: immigration policy and access of international students and scholars to our campuses, and to scientific meetings, would come into question; restrictions on publication and open scientific dialog about topics of potential use by terrorists would be proposed; and safeguards and restrictions on the use in our campus laboratories of potentially dangerous materials, especially biological agents, would be established.

Indeed, each of these concerns became real in the months following 9/11. The passage of the USA PATRIOT Act in late October 2001, as well as various executive orders, affected both immigration policy and raised the issue of limited access to what were termed *sensitive areas of study*. The Student and Exchange Visitor Information System (SEVIS), which tracks basic information about foreign students and scholars, was upgraded and expanded at a highly accelerated pace. International students, scholars, and visitors to the United States were subjected to new reviews, interviews, delays, and much more frequent denials of visas. Ill-defined terms like *sensitive but unclassified* appeared more frequently in federal research contracts. The Bioterrorism Preparedness and Response Act of 2002 established a framework for protecting certain pathogens, referred to as *select agents*, from misuse. The editors of a large group of important journals in the life sciences established a self-policing mechanism to restrict publication of information that might be key to the development of unusually dangerous mechanisms of bioterrorist attacks.

The issue before us became, and remains, how can our nation and our universities be *both* secure and open? The goal we in research universities had to pursue, and must continue to pursue, is the establishment of sound federal policy.

These complicated issues are not without precedent. In 1947, as our federal research policy was developing on the foundation of Vannevar Bush's report *Science—The Endless Frontier* and on the subsequent work of William T. Golden, concerns about security in the face of the Soviet threat and the spread of communism led President Truman's Scientific Research Board to eloquently state: "Strict military security in the narrow sense is not entirely consistent with the broader requirements of national security. To be secure as a Nation we must maintain a climate conducive to the full flowering of free inquiry. However important secrecy about military weapons may be, the fundamental discoveries of researchers must circulate freely to have full beneficial effect. Security regulations therefore should be applied only when strictly necessary and then limited to specific instruments, machines or processes. They should not attempt to cover basic principles of fundamental knowledge."

Beginning just two years later, and extending into the 1950s, we faced the terrible intrusions and excesses of the McCarthy-era House Un-American Activities Committee, whose history we know all too well. Nonetheless, federal science policy proceeded forward with a reasonably straightforward framework for the military classification of certain scientific and technological matters, especially those associated with nuclear weapons. Most classified work was conducted in federal weapons laboratories, but some such work was conducted on various campuses.

In 1980 concerns about critical defense-related technologies leaking to the Soviet Union became a matter of high-profile concern to the Department of Defense and Congress. Universities were seen as prime targets for espionage and the disclosure of technological knowledge that our adversaries could use against us. Even the National Academies suspended bilateral exchanges for a period.[3]

In 1982 Executive Order 12356 broadened the authority of the government to classify defense-relevant information, but the order stated that "Basic scientific research information not clearly related to national security may not be classified." There was much debate about the interpretation of this sentence, and great uncertainty about how it would be implemented. An answer soon came. As an optics researcher, I remember vividly the community's discussions about a meeting of the Society of Photo-Optical Instrumentation Engineers (SPIE) in San Diego in August 1982. The talk was about the withdrawal, under government pressure and with less than ten days' notice, of the presentation of more than 150 technical papers on cryptography.

A debate raged, and numerous groups addressed these matters. The National Academy of Sciences and the National Research Council appointed a panel to study the issue.[4] They concluded that *security by secrecy* would inevitably weaken U.S. technological capabilities, and that it is not possible to restrict international scientific communication without disrupting domestic scientific communication. But this panel did recommend that controls be devised for *gray areas.*

During this same period, Richard DeLauer became under secretary of defense for research and engineering. He took great interest in this topic and exerted quietly effective leadership, especially by co-chairing with Donald Kennedy, then president of Stanford, the DOD-University Forum. Largely on the basis of their work, a move to elucidate a *sensitive but unclassified* category was dropped, and DeLauer issued a memorandum to the Armed Services and the Defense Advanced Research Projects Agency (DARPA) emphasizing that university research should either be classified or unclassified.[5]

DeLauer's efforts and memorandum became the basis for President Reagan's September 1985 National Security Decision Directive 189 (NSDD 189), which states:

> It is the policy of this Administration that, to the maximum extent possible, the products of fundamental research remain unrestricted . . . that where the national security requires control, the mechanism for control of information generated during federally-funded fundamental research in science, technology, and engineering at colleges, universities and laboratories is classification.
>
> Each federal government agency is responsible for: a) determining whether classification is appropriate prior to the award of a research grant, contract, or cooperative agreement and, if so, controlling the research results through standard classification procedures; b) periodically reviewing all research grants, contracts, or cooperative agreements for potential classification.
>
> No restrictions may be placed upon the conduct or reporting of federally-funded fundamental research that has not received national security classification, except as provided in applicable U.S. Statutes.

After 1985 the general issue of export controls in academic settings more or less lay dormant for over a decade, but by the late 1990s it was gathering steam again. Universities began to be told that the conduct of basic scientific research that utilized satellite systems, and in some cases computer systems, was off-limits to foreign students and to collaborative efforts with other countries, even close friends like Japan. If non-U.S. citizens worked on projects and came into contact with certain specialized equipment, the knowledge they gained was considered a *deemed export* (the verbal, written, electronic, and/or visual disclosure of export-controlled scientific and technical information to foreign nationals in the United States), and they were either barred from the contact or required to pass certain security reviews. Quiet, but essentially fruitless, discussions between university leaders and federal officials ensued, and in several instances universities turned down such contracts rather than accept restrictions on their students.

Not all threats to scientific and technological openness have been based on national-security concerns. During the 1980s and early 1990s, many manufacturing-based U.S. corporations found themselves unable to compete well in global markets. Japan in particular had eclipsed us in the ability to manufacture goods with high quality, efficiency, and throughput and with short product cycle times. Japanese engineers and businesspeople learned a lot about U.S. products and innovations, but they also developed business processes, factories, and approaches to total quality management that strongly outperformed us.

Somewhat predictably, there was pressure to raise the ramparts—through classical trade protectionism and through shielding our technological innovations. Because MIT had long-standing good relationships with Japanese companies, we came under strong criticism. In 1989 the House Government Operations Committee's Subcommittee on Human Resources held a very contentious hearing, during which MIT president Paul Gray was roundly criticized, in essence for giving away America's crown jewels of technology through exchange activities with Japanese companies and scholars. In 1992 a U.S. senator circulated a graphic image entitled "The Circle of Shame." It depicted technical knowledge being passed from MIT to Japanese students, only to be developed by them into products marketed to damage the U.S. economy. The U.S. intelligence community was increasingly focused on international industrial espionage. Universities across the country were criticized for their increasing populations of international, and especially Asian, students. There were strong pushes to bar international students from university research programs.

Of course, much of the economic threat was very real. Japanese policies did not result in a level playing field for our automotive and consumer-electronics industries. But Japan also had the advantage of building new industries and "green field" factories, unencumbered by aging plants and equipment, tired management practices, and executives who had grown unused to serious competition. Ironically, in the end the United States learned a great deal about management and quality control from Japan. While there is no way to quantify this, I suspect that we gained more value from these management innovations than they did from learning about our technology. Indeed, by the early 1990s universities were criticized, with some good reason, for not having been ahead of the curve in teaching their business and engineering students about total quality management and new approaches to product development in the first place.

In any event, the openness of our universities survived these stresses more or less unscathed. Subsequently many of our large industries transformed themselves into efficient and high-quality manufacturers, and the entrepreneurial sector led us into strong economic growth in the late 1990s. Most of the criticism of international students and connections then abated.

Predictably, however, following the collapse of the dot-com economic bubble, national paranoia about leaking technological knowledge and mild xenophobia recurred. In fact, it was, and is, more a case of policy schizophrenia. Both before and after 9/11 the dominant reason for rejecting students applying for visas to study in the United States appears to have been *immigrant intent*—that is, the government was afraid that these prospective students would stay in the United States after they completed their studies. Yet many policy makers simultaneously decried the fact that increasing numbers of international students who had studied here were returning to their countries of origin to contribute to the development of their economies and universities rather than to ours.

Thus for five decades the international population of our graduate programs in science, engineering, and management has grown steadily. Science has had a strong culture of international cooperation and communication throughout this period. As in industry, higher education and research have increased their global reach and international interactions. But periodic episodes of federal interference with scientific communication and concerns about international students have occurred. These have been driven both by Cold War security concerns and by commercial concerns that have tended to be countercyclical to the strength of our economy.

With this historical context, let me return to the debates, issues, and accomplishments regarding universities and national security in the post-9/11 era. The most visible issues have revolved around the policy and practice of granting visas to foreign students planning to study in U.S. universities. Since the fall of 2001 this has been a complicated mixture of legitimate concerns, overreaction, bureaucratic foibles, risk aversion, antiquated systems, good intentions, bad policies, heart-rending personal experiences, and, finally, slow but steady improvement.

At the heart of most concerns about visas for students and scholars are three factors—fundamental immigration law, security reviews, and tracking systems. The legal basis for U.S. visitor-visa policies is Sec. 214(b) of the Immigration and Nationality Act of 1952, which requires visitors to prove to the satisfaction of a consular officer that they will not remain in the United States after completing the course of study or other specific activity for which they wish to be admitted. In other words, visitors must have ensured *nonimmigrant status*. Since 9/11, our embassies and consulates all over the world have attempted to apply this law rigorously to every applicant, despite the fact that it is an essentially impossible task.

The federal government maintains a Technology Alert List (TAL) itemizing areas of study, research, and devices that could result in the violation of laws prohibiting the export of goods, technology, or information sensitive to national security or economic competition. If an interviewing consular officer suspects that an applicant's proposed visit is related to something on the TAL, or otherwise might have national-security implications, the application is sent to Washington for a review called *Visa Mantis*. Another level of review, called *Visa CONDOR*, is conducted when a visa applicant's country of origin is considered by the State Department to sponsor terrorism, or if for any other reason concerns about terrorism are raised. These reviews have frequently resulted in major delays in issuing visas.

Finally, once they are in the United States, foreign students and visitors are entered into a computerized database, the Student and Exchange Visitor Information System (SEVIS). The basic purpose of SEVIS is to verify that foreign students are pursuing their intended course of study at a certified institution. Most SEVIS information was already required prior to 9/11 and is basically very simple "directory information." The system itself, however, was woefully inadequate prior to 9/11, and its updating and restructuring were very complicated, time-consuming, and expensive, and introduced substantial delays and problems for students and institutions for several years following 9/11.

The rigorous and collective application of these laws, reviews, and systems has had unfortunate results. As a nation, we have done great, though hopefully still reversible, harm to both our image and our reality because we substantially pulled back the celebrated American welcome mat—suddenly withdrawing it and then slowly rolling it back in the general direction of the prominent position it had occupied in previous decades. Personally, I don't feel a lot safer at night because of all this.

My colleagues Alice Gast and Danielle Guichard-Ashbrook, MIT's vice president for research and associate graduate dean, respectively, summarized the situation succinctly as they contemplated pending congressional discussion of student and scholar visa issues in 2005:

> The cumulative effects of the post 9/11 visa policies have harmed our national reputation as the premier environment to pursue forefront research in an open and productive environment. There is a growing perception among our foreign colleagues and the foreign press that the U.S. is no longer a welcoming place to study. The visa processes, including interviews, fingerprints and pictures, treat our international students and scholars as potential threats, and many of them are questioning the need to come to the U.S. under such conditions. They are actively exploring

increasingly attractive options, in Australia, Europe and Asia. We will need to compete for the best international students in ways we never had to before. This competition will require government and university attention.

International students apply to DOS [the Department of State] for student visas based on much documented evidence confirming their academic acumen and their personal backgrounds. Upon entry to the U.S., they are fingerprinted and photographed. Once in the U.S., they are tracked through SEVIS on everything from marital status to change in degree level. They cannot get social security numbers or drivers licenses without the SSA [Social Security Administration] confirming their immigration status with Immigration and Customs Enforcement, known as ICE. They cannot be employed without explicit permission from their academic institutions and/or Customs and Immigration Services (CIS). They need our signatures on their immigration documents in order to re-enter the U.S. from a trip abroad. Between academic and federal databases such as SEVIS, there is a surfeit of trackable data on these foreign nationals. Given this, one might ask why additional bureaucratic processes are needed for an overwhelmingly compliant and low risk group of foreign nationals. Among our international students and scholars, it promulgates ambivalence about studying in the U.S.[6]

These matters, together with larger geopolitical considerations, have created a far less favorable opinion of the United States in much of the world than that to which we are accustomed. This is demonstrated dramatically by a poll conducted last year. In 2005 the Pew Research Center asked 17,000 people from sixteen countries: "Suppose a young person who wanted to leave this country asked you to recommend where to go to lead a good life—what country would you recommend?" In only one of the sixteen countries (India) was the United States the most frequently recommended country.

The effects of all this on our universities have been substantial. Between 2003 and 2004 the number of international students applying to U.S. graduate programs fell by 32 percent, and the number of such students admitted to graduate programs declined by 18 percent.[7] This major shift is not yet fully understood, however. Although unhappiness with U.S. policy and perceived attitudes is clearly a major factor in this sudden shift, competition from universities in other parts of the world, economic factors, and even fear of moving about in a troubled world are undoubtedly in play as well.

Universities in other parts of the world see a clear opportunity to take advantage of this situation. While we are obsessed with trying to guess which student applicants might do us harm or return home to start an entrepreneurial business, others say, in effect, "If the United States doesn't want you, come here, where you are welcome." For example, several outstanding European universities are shifting their instructional language to English to better appeal to students from other parts of the world. This perception also negatively affects our faculty recruiting.

Despite the frustrating nature of these matters, many people of good will in corners of the State Department, the Department of Homeland Security, and the White House understand the damage being done and have worked hard to keep the nation both secure and open. Systems have slowly improved, times required for security reviews have been reduced, and more personnel have been hired to interview and process applications in consulates around the world. While he was secretary of state,

Colin Powell issued instructions that gave visa-processing priority to students and scholars. More recently, the time period during which an international student or scholar can leave and reenter the country without having to reapply for a visa has been extended from one to up to four years, once they have received Visa Mantis clearance. The systems are becoming smoother and more efficient, although numerous problems continue to exist. This is important progress, but it certainly has not completely restored our global image as open and welcoming. International participation in scientific meetings held in the United States has declined, because some scientists dislike what they consider to be negative attitudes and undue complexity, or because visa applications could not be processed in time. International collaborative efforts are suffering for the same reasons. This remains a serious problem.

There are deeper trends that I worry about even more. These have to do with restrictions on research and scientific communication. Some are mind-boggling. Consider the actions of the Treasury Department's Office of Foreign Assets Control (OFAC). In 2003 OFAC addressed the publication in American scientific journals, specifically those of the Institute of Electrical and Electronics Engineers (IEEE), of papers by authors who reside in countries that we consider to threaten our interests or harbor terrorists. Their interpretation of the law was that journals could publish such papers, but they could not edit them or transmit reviewer's comments, because editing manuscripts would constitute commerce with that nation. This is truly in the spirit of *Alice in Wonderland*. Eventually OFAC reversed the IEEE ruling, but uncertainties about the generality of its action remain. OFAC currently is refusing to grant a license to MIT architecture students to travel to Cuba as part of a studio course.

Closely related to OFAC and export-control regimes—and far more widespread—is the increasing appearance of national-security-based restrictive clauses in federal research contracts with universities. Typical restrictions include invoking a clause from the Federal Acquisition Regulations (FAR) that absolutely prohibits publication of research unless approved by the government; ad hoc restrictions to require nonstandard agency reviews of publications; restricting the involvement of foreign nationals in research or requiring special security reviews of them; and limiting distribution of data or reports, even though they are not classified. Such restrictions are at odds with the bright line of classification spelled out in NSDD 189. As discussed above, NSDD 189 was adopted in 1985; however, in the fall of 2001 the president's national security advisor, Condoleezza Rice, reiterated in a letter to former secretary of defense Harold Brown that it remained operative, stating that "the policy on the transfer of scientific, technical, and engineering information set forth in NSDD 189 shall remain in effect, and we will ensure that the policy is followed."[8]

This puts universities squarely on the line. It is our choice to accept or reject contracts that include such restrictions. It is essential in my view that we be certain that on our campuses contracting officers carefully scrutinize contracts for such troublesome clauses, and that we have specific processes for review and decision about whether to accept them. Frequently universities that have pushed back and carried the discussion higher in sponsoring agencies have succeeded in getting such clauses removed. In cases where this is not possible, some institutions have rejected the contracts, whereas others have accepted them. Informal discussions among twenty public and private research universities that are diverse in size and location leads me to estimate that about two-thirds of the troublesome clauses they encounter are negotiated out or rejected. Most of these are in fact negotiated out through multiple discussions with the agencies over a period of months.

I personally believe that the default for universities should be to reject such clauses. They represent a slippery slope that could lead to serious erosion of the basic values of openness at U.S. universities and could harm the fundamental processes of scientific inquiry. I believe that we best serve our nation by adhering to these values and processes. It also is my view that we teach our students by how we react to these sometimes difficult situations.

Concerns intensified in 2004 when the inspector generals of the Departments of Commerce, Defense, and Energy completed a review of university adherence to export-control regulations. This review was required by the National Defense Authorization Act of 2000. Although the resulting reports noted no violations, they did disclose that neither the federal agencies nor the universities were fully cognizant of the full spectrum of export-control regulations, including those covering deemed exports. With deemed exports, the presumption is that conveying export-controlled scientific and technical information to a foreign national in the United States is equivalent to exporting the information to a foreign national outside the United States. Following the inspector generals' reports, the Department of Commerce issued new draft regulations. As a consequence of the draft regulations, universities are facing possible requirements to seek licenses for legally admitted foreign students, scholars, faculty, and staff to have access to technology on how to operate, install, maintain, repair, overhaul, and refurbish controlled equipment within the United States. If adopted, these regulations would inevitably lead to partitioning and segregation of equipment and materials on our campuses, with attendant systems for requiring badges, processing, and monitoring that would fundamentally change the nature of our institutions. These changes would reduce our value to the nation and to society because openness and interaction are essential to the conduct of fundamental research, and because the work of our universities in education and research is absolutely essential to our nation's long-term economic strength, health, quality of life, and—most assuredly—*security*. Fortunately, Secretary of State Rice and others high in the federal administration have recently taken cognizance of this issue, and there is reason to hope that it can be resolved or at least that its negative consequences can be substantially attenuated.

CONCLUSION

These are complicated times as we try to balance very real security concerns against the critically important openness of our institutions—openness to international students, scholars, and faculty members, as well as the openness of scientific inquiry and communication. There has been considerable respectful and productive dialog between our community and the federal government on many of the issues that have arisen, but we are not out of the woods. Continued vigilance and change will be required if we are to sustain the world leadership of our educational and research institutions. The lessons of history confirm that openness is a great contributor to the security of our nation and world in the long run, and must be preserved.

FOUR

The Emerging Global Meta-University

*Higher Education and Scholarship
in the Age of the Internet*

Even as we face and resolve the thorny issue of balancing security and openness to sustain our campuses as great magnets for the brightest minds from around the world, modern information and communication technologies have fundamentally altered what it means to be an open scholarly or educational community.[1] At the same time, India, China, and other countries are making strong investments to bring their research universities to world-class status. Strong forces and great opportunities are extant in higher education. How will the use of so-called educational technology play out? What will be the nature of the globalization of higher education? Will the Age of the Internet and what lies beyond it fundamentally reshape education and research? Are residential universities dying dinosaurs, or models to be propagated further?

My personal assessment of these matters is made in the context of two admitted biases. First, I remain hopelessly in love with the residential university—with Clark Kerr's multiversity.

Teaching is a fundamentally human activity, and it is difficult for me to envision anything better than the magic that happens when a group of smart, motivated, and energetic young men and women live and learn together for a period of years in a lively and intense university environment. Second, years ago I read a book by Princeton's Gerard O'Neill in which he looked back over the centuries at what futurists of each period had predicted and then compared their predictions with what had actually occurred.[2] The primary lesson from this study is that the rate of technological progress is almost always dramatically underpredicted, and the rate of social progress is almost always dramatically overpredicted. I share this view.

What I envision, therefore, is a way in which relatively stable and conservative institutions will develop enormous synergies through the use of ever-expanding technological tools. Indeed, this is already happening in profound ways.

INFORMATION TECHNOLOGY
AND HIGHER EDUCATION

Computers, of course, have had a strong influence on higher education since the 1960s, starting out as specialized tools in science, engineering, and mathematics, and then propagating across the humanities, arts, and social sciences, as well as to business, law, and medicine. During the late 1990s, following the development of the World Wide Web and accelerated by the ever-decreasing prices of storage and processing, educators everywhere began to see information technology as a transformative force. This coincided with the dot-com era in the world of business, so attention quickly turned to how universities could teach large numbers of students at a distance, and how they could realize financial profits by doing so. Journalists, critics, and many of our own faculty concluded that classroom teaching in lecture format was doomed. Economies of scale could be garnered and many more people could afford to obtain advanced educations via digital means. For-profit distance education was assumed to be the emerging coin of our realm. University faculty and administrators across the country wrestled over the ownership of intellectual property when a professor's course was made available electronically.

Profit-making arms of some major universities, such as Fathom.Com at Columbia, were formed; providers like the University of Phoenix rapidly expanded; and adult-focused universities like Strayer moved online. The Western Governors Conference established a distance-education program as a collective effort to offer degrees and certificates through online courses in business, education, and information technology.

The model that was proposed over and again for higher education was "find the best teacher of a given subject, record his or her lectures, and sell them in digital form." There is an appealing logic to this proposition, and I very much believe that there are important roles for this kind of teaching tool, but the image of students everywhere sitting in front of a box listening to the identical lecture is one that repels me. It struck me as odd that many of the same critics who decried the lack of personal attention given students on our campuses seemed eager to move to this model. Nonetheless, the dominant proposition was that a university should project itself beyond its campus boundaries to teach students elsewhere.

In the meantime many other teaching and learning innovations were introduced on campuses. Increasingly effective computer-based tools for language acquisition were developed. Online journals were published. Computer simulations were used in subjects ranging from fluid mechanics to theater stage design. Studio-style instruction with heavy use of computational tools was refined. As Murray Gel-Man likes to say, "The sage on the stage was being replaced by the guide at the side." Multiple institutions shared large scientific databases. Massive search engines made information available to anyone with a Web browser, and this quietly and quickly revolutionized the work of many students and faculty. (It also introduced new complexities and issues of ethics by blurring definitions of *original work* and *plagiarism*.) Informal electronic learning communities formed, both within and among universities. Distinguished architects located on multiple continents used video and Web interactions to come together as juries for architecture studio projects. In other words, information technology, usually through increasingly large accumulations of modest, local activities, was transforming much of what we do on our campuses. It was bringing the world to the students on our campuses, as well as projecting our activities outward.

At the Andrew W. Mellon Foundation, William C. Bowen and his colleagues developed ideas about how to empower large numbers of scholars and institutions through a combination of technology and economy of scale that in 1990 coalesced in the establishment of JSTOR. JSTOR makes available digital copies of scholarly journals in the liberal arts, sciences, and humanities for modest annual fees scaled to institutional size. JSTOR currently serves 2,600 institutions, almost half of which are outside the United States, and archives 580 scholarly journals from more than 360 publishers. It helps individual scholars conducting advanced study and research at major universities. It also enables small liberal-arts colleges with very modest resources to collectively or individually mount courses and research programs in areas of the arts and sciences for which they could not have afforded appropriate library collections. In 2001 the Mellon Foundation launched a second major venture, ARTstor, which uses a similar approach to provide institutions with a huge, carefully developed archive of high-quality digital images of great works of art. By 2006 ARTstor will include 500,000 images.

In my view, JSTOR was a particularly important development in bringing the power of the Internet, and of sharing large digital archives, to humanistic scholars and students in a wide array of colleges and universities. It pointed toward a new type of *openness* in higher education.

MIT OPENCOURSEWARE

In 1997 I prepared for that inevitable duty of a university president—leading a capital campaign. Our resource-development staff had organized a dozen dinners, each in a different city, for thoughtful prospective donors and alumni, with whom I would engage in dialog about MIT's future. At each dinner, the first question asked of me was: "What is MIT going to do about information technology and distance learning?" My answer was always some variant of "I don't know." But the answer soon came from our faculty.

Our provost, Bob Brown, had appointed a task force to explore this question, building on the earlier work of the MIT Council on Educational Technology. Frankly, the bias going into this exercise was toward some sort of profit-generating production of educational modules on up-to-the-minute engineering and scientific topics that would be of particular interest to our alumni and to high-level engineers and managers in corporations with which we have research partnerships. The task force worked diligently, exploring various concepts and models and even studying the business plans of a large number of for-profit distance-learning organizations. They concluded that in the context of advanced higher education, distance learning would be complicated, highly competitive, and unlikely to turn a profit. This sowed the seed of a beautiful idea—why not just make our detailed educational materials broadly available on the Web, free of charge?

From this beginning, the MIT OpenCourseWare (OCW) initiative was born. With generous financial support from the Mellon and Hewlett Foundations, MIT pledged to make available on the Web, free of charge to teachers and learners everywhere, the substantially complete teaching materials from virtually all of the approximately two thousand subjects we teach on our campus. For most subjects, these materials include a syllabus, course calendar, well-formatted and detailed lecture notes, exams, problem sets and solutions, and lab and project plans; in a few cases, they also include video lectures. The materials have been cleared for third-party intellectual property and are available to users under a Creative Commons license so that they can be used, distributed, and modified for noncommercial purposes.

OpenCourseWare is a new, open form of publication. It is not teaching, and it is not the offering of courses or degrees. It is an exercise in openness, a catalyst for change, and an adventure. It is an adventure because it is a free-flowing, empowering, and potentially democratizing force, so we do not know in advance the uses to which it will be put. Indeed, users' stories and unusual paths are almost as numerous as our users themselves. An Arizona high-school teacher motivates and supervises group study of MIT OCW computer-science materials within his after-school artificial-intelligence club. A group of then-unemployed programmers in Silicon Valley used MIT OCW materials to master advanced computer languages, upgrading their skills when the job market became very tight. An educator at Al-Mansour University College in Baghdad utilized MIT OCW aeronautics and astronautics course material in his air-traffic-control research. The computer-science department of a university in Legon, Ghana, is updating its entire curriculum, using MIT OCW materials to help benchmark and revise its courses. In another country, an underground university based largely on MIT OCW educates young men and women who, because of their religion, are forbidden to attend universities. Heavy use is made of MIT OCW by almost 70 percent of the students on our own campus to review courses they have taken in the past, to reinforce the classes they are currently taking, and to explore other areas of study.

By fall 2006 we had mounted the materials for about 1,550 subjects from thirty-three academic disciplines in all five of our schools, with 80 percent of our faculty participating. The site averages more than one million visits per month, with the average visitor using almost ten HTML pages per visit. Visitors are located on every continent. Forty-three percent of the traffic is from North America, 20 percent from East Asia, and 16 percent from Western Europe. The remaining 20 percent of users are distributed across Latin America, Eastern Europe, the Middle

East, the Pacific Region, and Sub-Saharan Africa. International usage is growing rapidly. Roughly 15 percent of OCW users are educators, and almost half of their usage is directly for course and curriculum development. One-third of the users are students complementing a course they are taking at another college or university, or simply expanding their personal knowledge. Almost half of the users are self-learners.

OpenCourseWare seems counterintuitive in a market-driven world, but it represents the intellectual generosity that faculties of great American universities have demonstrated in many ways over the years.[3] In an innovative manner, it expresses a belief that education can be advanced around the world by constantly widening access to information and pedagogical organization, and by inspiring others to participate. In my view, the establishment of OpenCourseWare is consistent with MIT's particular history and values. Let me explain.

As noted in the introduction to this book, in the late 1950s and 1960s MIT played a prominent role in launching the engineering science revolution. This role originated during World War II, when MIT operated the Radiation Laboratory for the U.S. Army. The Rad Lab, a joint effort between the United States and Great Britain, brought together a remarkable group of physicists, mathematicians, and engineers to work in a concerted manner to develop radar into practical systems for use in the war effort, which proved to be extremely important to the Allied victory. When the war ended, the government did something that seems unimaginable today. It actually closed down this successful lab, whose mission was then complete. But before they turned off the lights and locked the doors, they funded key staff for six months to record the technical essence of their work.

The twenty-seven volumes that documented their work had a greater significance; they formed the basis for a new approach to the practice of electrical engineering, and indeed engineering more broadly.[4] This approach was to move engineering away from being primarily a phenomenological and experience-based "handbook" profession to one more centrally based on scientific first principles.

This stimulated an educational revolution, particularly under the vision and leadership of engineering dean Gordon Brown. Subjects were redeveloped on a base of science, and new teaching materials—lecture notes, problem sets, and experiments—were generated throughout MIT. In due course, much of this was formalized as published textbooks and textbook series. But what really propagated the engineering science revolution was the rapidly increasing number of engineering PhDs educated at MIT joining faculties of universities and colleges all across the country. They brought with them the new lecture notes, draft textbooks, problem sets, and laboratory experiments. These new professors adapted the MIT teaching materials to their new environments. They added to them, subtracted from them, and used them to teach at varying paces. This merged into developing programs at many universities, and before long the nature and quality of engineering education was elevated across the country. Of course, many other leading institutions, like Stanford, Illinois, Wisconsin, and Berkeley, contributed greatly to this rapid evolution.

All this sprang to my mind when Bob Brown told me that the task force on educational technology intended to recommend giving away all of MIT's course materials online. Although I was not educated at MIT, the work there had directly impacted my undergraduate education at West Virginia University and my graduate education at the University of Michigan. So it seemed instantly clear that in 1999 a well-developed initiative could have a similar impact worldwide, at "Internet speed," and without recent MIT graduates as intermediaries. I became an instant and passionate advocate for the initiative that became MIT OpenCourseWare.

AN OPEN-COURSEWARE MOVEMENT

As our faculty had hoped, today there is an emerging open-courseware movement. Indeed, we know of sixty open-courseware initiatives in the United States, China, Japan, France, Spain, Portugal, and Brazil. Thirty more initiatives are being planned, in South Africa, the United Kingdom, Russia, and elsewhere. Consistent with our open philosophy, MIT OCW has actively worked to encourage and assist this movement, especially through the OpenCourseWare Consortium.

Here in the United States, the University of Michigan, Utah State University, the Johns Hopkins University School of Public Health, and Tufts University's Health Sciences and Fletcher School of Diplomacy all have established open-courseware efforts. Here I use the term *open courseware* to denote substantial, comprehensive, carefully managed, easily accessed, searchable, Web-based collections of teaching materials for entire courses presented in a common format.

In this emerging open-courseware movement, it is not only the teaching materials that are shared. We have also implemented and actively encouraged the sharing with other institutions of know-how, software, and other tools developed by MIT OCW.

I find particularly visionary the Sofia (from "Sharing of free intellectual assets") project of the Foothill-De Anza Community College District in Los Altos, California, for which the Hewlett Foundation has provided important support. Sofia extends the open-courseware movement to a different, and extremely important, sector of education—the community colleges. It is still in a pilot phase, but it seems to me that the curricula of community colleges—which serve highly motivated populations, many of whom have quite focused interests and modest budgets of time and money—are well-suited to an open-courseware approach.

A very different example is China Open Resources for Education (CORE), which is translating MIT OCW courses into Mandarin and making them available across China. In return, CORE is beginning to make Chinese courses available and translating them into English. Another MIT OCW partner, Universia, a consortium of 840 institutions in the Spanish-speaking world, translates MIT OCW subjects into Spanish and makes them available. Finally, Utah State University's Center for Open and Sustainable Learning is doing outstanding research on open learning, materials, and software.

My point here is that openly accessible resources can be used in their entirety, in part, at any pace, and can be added to, deleted from, or modified to fit a teacher's or learner's purpose and context.

How will open courseware evolve in the future? Will its evolution continue to be largely by replication of the MIT OCW model in other institutions? Will it grow, Linux-like, into a single entity with continual improvements by educators and learners around the world? Or will it be replaced by other developments? I do not know the answer to this question beyond the next few years, but I do consider it to be part of a broader class of open-source materials.

OPEN ARCHIVING, INDEXING, AND PUBLISHING

The seminal development of JSTOR has been followed by several other open-access projects for archiving, indexing, and publishing scholarly work. Examples include the Google Print Library Project, the Million Book Project, and DSpace.

Google has engaged several of the world's great libraries—the New York Public Library and those of Harvard University, the University of Michigan, the University of Oxford, and Stanford University—with the stated goal to "digitally scan books from their collections so that users worldwide can search them in Google." The Print Library Project is a book-finding initiative, not a book-reading one: if a book is out of copyright, the entire book is accessible; otherwise, one can view snippets of the book, or a few of its pages, and obtain information about purchasing it.

Another major digital-archiving initiative is the Million Book Project, a collaboration of Carnegie Mellon University, the Online Computer Library Center (OCLC), as well as government and academic institutional partners in China and India. Its goal is to create a free-to-read, searchable digital library. This initiative is notable for its highly international collection. As of last fall, it included more than 600,000 books, of which 170,000 are from India, 420,000 are from China, and 20,000 are from Egypt; 135,000 of the books are in English.

DSpace has a different goal than the archiving projects discussed above: it is a digital platform designed to make available the scholarly output of a single university, including preprints, technical reports, working papers, theses, conference reports, images, and so on. This is the stuff of working scholarship, at the opposite end of the spectrum from out-of-copyright books and journals. MIT has worked in alliance with the Hewlett-Packard Corporation to create this archive, and to establish the DSpace Federation to promote and enable institutions to establish similar repositories using freely available open-source software. DSpace has been adopted by at least 150 institutions located on every continent except Antarctica. Many of these institutions contribute to the ongoing improvement of the open-source DSpace platform code.

There is an additional, and potentially very important, dimension to the open movement—the publication of open-access journals. The first major foray into this domain is the Public Library of Science (PLoS), founded in 2000. This initiative, spearheaded by Harold Varmus, CEO of the Sloan-Kettering Memorial Cancer Center, and professors Patrick Brown and Michael Eisen of Stanford and Berkeley, respectively, publishes open-access journals in biology and medicine, and promotes open access within the scientific community.

PLoS utilizes a broad definition of open access: "everything published in PLoS journals is immediately available online for free. Read it, print it, copy it, distribute it—all use is fair use, so long as the original authors and source are credited." Currently PLoS publishes five journals: *PLoS Biology*, *PLoS Medicine*, *PLoS Computational Biology*, *PLoS Genetics*, and *PLoS Pathogens*. The vision of PLoS is very similar to that of the open-courseware movement—that we should utilize the empowering properties of the Internet to make scientific information quickly available as a public good.

The Howard Hughes Medical Institute and the Welcome Trust encourage the open-publication movement by providing publication costs for researchers whose work they have sponsored if it is published in open-access journals.

ISSUES FACING THE OPEN-ACCESS MOVEMENT

There are at least four fundamental issues to be addressed if open-access materials are to reach their full potential for use by scholars, teachers, students, and self-learners: intellectual-property rights, quality control, cost, and bandwidth.

Intellectual-property issues are clearly inherent in archiving projects, because the publishers of books and journals mostly own the copyrights. The resolution usually is some variant of a time delay, such as open access to a book only after the copyright has expired, or open access to a journal issue only after some fixed number of years has elapsed since its publication. In the case of open-courseware projects, nettlesome third-party intellectual-property issues arise when a professor makes use of a graph or certain types of excerpts from books or journal articles. Crediting a figure or excerpt from a publisher's product would seem to me to be great free advertising. After all, companies pay huge amounts of money for a glimpse of their product to appear in a movie or television program. Some publishers agree, but many do not. In any event, publishers' approaches vary, and careful screening of materials for intellectual property is a time-consuming and expensive aspect of creating and sustaining open-courseware projects.

Of course, some faculty may be reluctant to have their teaching materials freely available online, because they plan to use them as the basis for a textbook or other commercial dissemination. It was extremely satisfying for me to observe that this was a very minor issue when the MIT faculty undertook to establish MIT OCW.

Quality control—that is, certification of the accuracy and appropriateness of scholarly and teaching materials on the Web—is a fundamental issue. The Web is a Wild West of information that has little or no vetting or peer review. The imprimatur and standards of leading universities, professional organizations, and scholarly oversight groups therefore are of great value when they establish organizations devoted to open publication and archiving.

The production, maintenance, and distribution of materials on the Web have very real costs. In general, the more sophisticated the material and distribution are, the greater the costs. The societal value of freely available materials, and indeed the value of sharing materials among institutions, is substantial, but there still is a bottom line. I am passionate about keeping my own institution's open courseware without cost to users, but that is possible only through the generosity of foundations, in the first instance, and of corporate and individual partners and supporters in the longer run. MIT also has pledged to meet a fraction of the sustaining costs itself. Most major archives have a business plan in which there are user fees, but strong efforts have been made thus far to keep these as modest as possible, and to scale them to the size of the user institution.

Bandwidth is a very serious obstacle to one of the most attractive potentials of the open and nonprofit movements for scholarship and education—namely, its impact in the developing world.

Institution building and scholarship in these countries can be given a terrific boost from access to these materials. Yet to take the best advantage of the materials, easy access and interactive participation via broadband are very important.

Hopefully open-access activities will provide further stimulus for governments and nongovernmental organizations to increase the availability and lower the cost of high-bandwidth connectivity. This is key to bridging the digital divide. In the meantime MIT OCW has deployed seventy-six mirror sites on local university networks throughout the developing world as a promising alternative. A single mirror site at Makerere University in Uganda generates more traffic than the total traffic from Sub-Saharan Africa to the MIT OCW site on the World Wide Web.

The ease of use and interactivity of the Web make it the most attractive option for access to open courseware and archives. However, they are not necessarily the only option. Delivery of CDs could work in some instances, although the ease of updating, maintenance, and interactivity would suffer. The rapidly dropping cost of computer memory suggests another option. The amount of iPod memory per dollar is approximately doubling each year: in round numbers, a 20 gigabyte device cost $400 in 2004; that cost had dropped to $250 in 2005, and one could purchase 60 gigabytes for $450. Should this continue, by 2025 $400 might purchase 40 petabytes![5] In any event, this suggests another mechanism for delivering courseware and archival materials.

A NEXT STAGE: WEB-BASED LABORATORIES

I believe that it is likely that iLab, a project initially conceived and implemented by professor Jesus del Alamo of MIT, is a harbinger of the next stage of open access—the online laboratory. The principle is simple: computers today control most experiments; therefore experiments can be controlled from any distance through the Internet. This is not new in the world of research. Telescopes and other research instruments have often been operated from great distances. The idea behind iLab is to apply this concept to experiments used in teaching.

The iLab project was developed at MIT, in part through the support of the Microsoft iCampus initiative. In the first instance, it was designed to enable our own students to operate experimental equipment from their dorm rooms or other study venues that is, when and where they wanted. The slightly tongue-in-cheek motto was "If you can't come to the lab, the lab will come to you." Initially developed for microelectronics experiments, iLab has now expanded to teaching experiments involving chemical reactors, mechanical structures, heat exchangers, an instrumented flagpole, a shaker table, polymer crystallization, and a photovoltaic weather station.

Today iLab operates at institutions around the world: students in Britain, Greece, Sweden, Singapore, and Taiwan, for example, have all accessed iLab. Furthermore, the MIT group makes available iLab Shared Architecture, a tool kit of reusable modules and a set of standardized protocols for developing and managing online laboratories.

With support of the Carnegie Corporation of New York, iLab has expanded to cooperative development with three African universities (Makerere University, in Uganda; the University of Dar-es-Salaam, in Tanzania; and Obafemi Awolowo University, in Nigeria). Although in its infancy, I find the concept of students in a developing university that has very modest resources sitting at a laptop and running expensive experimental equipment at MIT, in industry, or at other universities truly exciting and educationally profound. Professor del Alamo and his colleagues are working toward a vision of OpeniLabs that someday may provide large-scale free and open access to on-line teaching laboratories.

CONCLUSION

The Age of the Internet and inexpensive information storage present remarkable opportunities for higher education and research in the United States and throughout the world. Day-to-day communication and data transfer among scholars and researchers now is totally dominated by Internet communications. Large, accessible scholarly archives like JSTOR and ARTstor are growing and heavily subscribed. The use of open courseware is developing in the United States, Asia, and Europe. To paraphrase the columnist Tom Friedman, the world is getting flat. I believe that openness and sharing of intellectual resources and teaching materials—not closely controlled point-to-point distance education—should emerge as a dominant ethos of global higher education.

In my view, a global meta-university is arising that will accurately characterize higher education a decade or two hence in much the same way that Clark Kerr's multiversity accurately characterized American research universities forty years ago. The rise of this meta-university of globally created and shared teaching materials, scholarly archives, and even laboratories could well be a dominant, democratizing force in the next few decades. It could grow to undergird and empower campuses everywhere, both rich and poor. Like the computer operating system Linux, knowledge creation and teaching at each university will be elevated by the efforts of a multitude of individuals and groups all over the world. It will rapidly adapt to the changing learning styles of students who have grown up in a computationally rich environment. The biggest potential winners are in developing nations.

This will happen because nation after nation is committed to enhancing and expanding higher education, and because there are global efficiencies and economies of scale to be had by sharing high-quality materials and systems that collectively are too expensive for each institution to develop independently. It will happen because this kind of sharing is not prescriptive. It is not paternalistic, and it need not be politically or culturally laden, because each individual institution, professor, or learner is free to use only those parts of the material he or she chooses and may adapt, modify, or add to it in fulfillment of the local needs, pedagogy, and context. Campuses will still be important, and universities will still compete for resources, faculty, students, and prestige, but they will do so on a digital platform of shared information, materials, and experience that will raise quality and access all around.

NOTES

INTRODUCTION

1. L. E. Grinter et al., "Report of the Committee on Evaluation of Engineering Education," *Engineering Education* 45 (September 1955): 25–60. A summary of this report, known as the Grinter Report, is reprinted in the *Journal of Engineering Education* 83, no. 1 (January 1994): 74–94.

1. GOVERNMENTS AND UNIVERSITIES

1. "Facts and Figures: College and University Endowments—741 College and University Endowments, 2003–04," *The Chronicle of Higher Education*, January 2005, http://chronicle.com/stats/endowments/.

2. Audrey Williams June, "Giving to Colleges Reaches a Plateau," *The Chronicle of Higher Education*, March 19, 2004: A25.

3. F. King Alexander quoted and American Association of University Professors (AAUP) salary data analyzed in Scott Smallwood, "The Price Professors Pay for Teaching at Public Universities," *The Chronicle*

of Higher Education, April 20, 2001: A18; http://chronicle.com/weekly/v47/i32/32a01801.htm.

4. John Vaughn, personal communication (with data from the Association of American Universities [AAU] Data Exchange), April 20, 2005.

5. "More State Universities Seek 'Privatizing' Route," *Chicago Sun-Times*, May 4, 2004: 13.

6. According to the University of California Annual Financial Report 2004–05, UCLA receives $609.2 million in state appropriations and contracts, and Berkeley receives $509.8 million. According to the University of Michigan Financial Report 2005, the state appropriation is $375 million, of which $320 million is for the Ann Arbor campus.

7. "Campuses with the Largest Enrollments, Fall 2002," *The 2005–6 Almanac of Higher Education*, special issue of *The Chronicle of Higher Education* 52, no. 1 (2006): 14.

8. James C. Garland, "How to Put College Back within Reach: Better Uses for State Education Dollars," *The Washington Post*, December 30, 2006: A27.

9. The National Center for Public Policy and Higher Education, *Policy Alert: Income of U.S. Workforce Projected to Decline if Education Doesn't Improve* (San Jose, CA, November 2005), http://www.highereducation.org/reports/pa_decline/index.shtml.

10. Vannevar Bush, *Science—The Endless Frontier: A Report to the President on a Program for Postwar Scientific Research* (1945; reprint, Washington, DC: National Science Foundation, 1990).

11. National Science Foundation, Division of Science Resources Statistics, *What Is the State Government Role in the R&D Enterprise?*, NSF 99-348, by John E. Jankowski (Arlington, VA, 1999), http://www.nsf.gov/statistics/nsf99348/text.htm.

12. State Science and Technology Institute and Battelle Memorial Institute, *Survey of State Research and Development Expenditures: Fiscal Year 1995* (Columbus, OH, September 1998).

2. INDUSTRY, PHILANTHROPY,
AND UNIVERSITIES

1. The Center on Philanthropy at Indiana University, Indianapolis, *Giving USA 2004: The Annual Report on Philanthropy for the Year 2003* (New York: Giving USA Foundation, 2004): 83, 87 (fig. 1).

2. National Science Foundation, Division of Science Resources Statistics, *Academic Research and Development Expenditures: Fiscal Year 2002*, NSF 04–330 (Arlington, VA, 2004): table B-1.

3. Remarks by Alan Greenspan at the International Understanding Award Dinner, Institute of International Education, New York, October 29, 2002, http://www.federalreserve.gov/boarddocs/Speeches/2002/20021029/default.htm.

4. See, for example, Government-University-Industry Research Roundtable, *Simplified and Standardized Model Agreements for University-Industry Cooperative Research* (Washington, DC: The National Academies Press, 1988).

5. Donald E. Stokes, *Pasteur's Quadrant: Basic Science and Technological Innovation* (Washington, DC: Brookings Institution Press, 1997).

6. See http://cybernation.com/quotationcenter/quoteauthor.php.

7. Council on Governmental Relations, *Finances of Research Universities* (Washington, DC, November 5, 2003), http://www.cogr.edu/.

8. National Association of College and University Business Officers, *2005 NACUBO Endowment Study* (Washington, DC, 2006). See also TIAA-CREF Institute, *Trends and Issues—2005 NACUBO Endowment Study: Highlights and Trends*, by Mimi Lord (New York, February 2006), http://www.tiaa-crefinstitute.org/research/trends/tr020106.html.

9. The Commonfund Institute, Addendum to *Sources of Endowment Growth at Colleges and Universities*, by G. P. Strehle (Wilton, CT, April 2005).

10. Council for Aid to Education, *Voluntary Support of Education 2004: National Estimates and Trends for Higher Education* (New York, 2005).

11. Ibid., 5.

12. T. Lewin, "Young Students Are New Cause for Big Donors," *The New York Times*, August 21, 2005, Section 1: 21.

13. See, for example, Gordon C. Winston, "Toward a Theory of Tuition: Prices, Peer Wages, and Competition in Higher Education," Williams Project on the Economics of Higher Education, Paper DP-65 (Williamstown, MA, January 2003), http://www.williams.edu/wpehe/abstracts.html#dp-65.

14. The College Board, *Trends in Student Aid 2004* (New York, 2004), http://www.collegeboard.com/prod_downloads/press/cost04/TrendsinStudentAid2004.pdf.

15. Much of this section is drawn from Charles M. Vest, *Pursuing the Endless Frontier: Essays on MIT and the Role of the Research University* (Cambridge, MA: The MIT Press, 2005): 271–74.

16. Michael McPherson, private communication, September 1, 2005.

17. 568 Presidents' Group, *The 568 Presidents' Group Consensus Methodology Policy Guidelines* (2000), http://568group.org/docs/cmmanual-non.pdf.

18. J.B. Lee, "How Do Students and Families Pay for College?" in J.E. King, ed., *ACE/Oryx Series on Higher Education* (Phoenix: The Oryx Press, 1999).

3. OPENNESS

1. U.S. Commission on National Security/21st Century, *Road Map for National Security: Imperative for Change* (Washington, DC: U.S. Government Printing Office, February 15, 2001): viii.

2. Ibid.: 30.

3. V.F. Weisskopf and R.R. Wilson, "United States–Soviet Scientific Exchanges" (editorial), *Science*, May 30, 1980: 977.

4. Committee on Science, Engineering, and Public Policy, *Scientific Communication and National Security*, by D.R. Corson et al. (Washington, DC: The National Academies Press, 1982).

5. I want to recognize Dr. John C. Crowley, formerly MIT's vice president for federal relations, for his research and strong contribution to my understanding of the history of these issues in the period 1947–85.

6. Alice P. Gast and Danielle Guichard-Ashbrook, private communication, May 17, 2005.

7. Committee on Science, Engineering, and Public Policy, *Policy Implications of International Graduate Students and Postdoctoral Scholars in the United States* (Washington, DC: The National Academies Press, 2005).

8. Condoleezza Rice, letter to Harold Brown, November 1, 2001, http://www.aau.edu/research/Rice11.1.01.html.

4. THE EMERGING GLOBAL META-UNIVERSITY

1. This chapter draws extensively on Charles M. Vest, "Open Content and the Emerging Global Meta-University," *EDUCAUSE Review* 41, no. 3 (May/June 2006): 18–30.

2. Gerard K. O'Neill, *2081: A Hopeful View of the Human Future* (New York: Simon and Schuster, 1981).

3. My colleagues and I are frequently asked—often skeptically—what other reasons, or submerged business model, lie behind the MIT decision to initiate OpenCourseWare, and how the decision was *really* made. The story is as simple as is related in this chapter. The institution has a proud altruistic streak, and most professors want their pedagogy and organization of knowledge and teaching to benefit as many people as possible, as long as there is no sacrifice of quality or "watering down" of their material. *Participation by faculty members in OpenCourseWare is voluntary.*

The provost, the chancellor, members of the committee that initiated the recommendation, or I visited every academic department to present the proposal, listen to reactions, discuss the views expressed, and understand the implicit *ground rules* under which they would be willing to participate. For example, the faculty appropriately insisted that the teaching materials of the entire institute be included—not just those of selected departments or schools. Through this process, a common understanding of OpenCourseWare developed, and there was far more than sufficient faculty enthusiasm for us to seek the necessary funds and staff and to publicly commit the institution to the initiative.

Of course, various benefits have accrued to MIT—some foreseen and some not. Our own students make extensive use of OCW materials. We gained the *first-mover advantage* in what is proving to be an important component of higher education, and it has generated a positive image and much goodwill for us. The reaction of our own alumni has been overwhelmingly enthusiastic.

4. *MIT Radiation Laboratory Series* (New York: McGraw-Hill, 1947–48).

5. R. Brooks, MIT Computer Science and Artificial Intelligence Laboratory, private communication, August 2005.

INDEX

Academic freedom, 8

Admissions, affirmative action in, 22–24

Advanced Research Projects Agency (ARPA), 26

Affirmative action, 21–24

African American engineering students, 23

Alexander, F. King, 15

Al-Mansour University College (Baghdad), use of OpenCourse-Ware, 97

Alumni: international, 58; philanthropy by, 54; support for financial aid, 68

American Society for Engineering Education, 3

Andrew W. Mellon Foundation, 94, 95; and OpenCourseWare project, 96

Armstrong, John, 41

ARTstor, 95, 108

Association of American Universities (AAU), 51

Bakke admission case, 22

Big Dig (Boston), 12

Biotechnology, university/corporate partnerships in, 45

Bioterrorism Preparedness and Response Act (2002), 75

Borders, national, openness of, 71

Boston: Big Dig at, 12; Route 128 corridor, 30

Bowen, William C., 94

Brown, Bob, 99

Brown, Gordon, 3, 99

Brown, Harold, 87

Brown, Patrick, 103

Bush, Vannevar, 27; *Science—The Endless Frontier*, 24–25, 40–41, 76

Business sector: cost effectiveness in, 60–61; social responsibility of, 53–54. *See also* Corporations

California: admissions policies in, 23–24; higher education in, 1–2, 10; Master Plan for Higher Education, 1–2; Proposition 209, 23

Caltech, budget reductions at, 12

Cambridge University, partnership with MIT, 48, 49

Carnegie Corporation (New York), 107

Carnegie Mellon University, open access projects of, 102

China, research universities of, 91

China Open Resources for Education (CORE), 101

"Circle of Shame" (graphic), 79

Cold War: federal science policy during, 76; national security during, 26, 76–77, 81

Colleges: community, 101; liberal-arts, 7

Columbia University, Fathom.Com program of, 93

Communication: digital, 32; technology of, 91

Communication, scientific, restrictions on, 86–87. *See also* Publication

Community colleges, use of open courseware, 101

Computer memory, cost of, 106, 108

Computer simulations, in teaching, 94

Cornell, public and private components of, 18

Corporations: commitment to university partnerships of, 45; effect on university missions, 46; partnerships with universities, 44–46; patent ownerships of, 47; philanthropy of, 54; research and development by, 43; support for research, 38–39

Defense Advanced Research Projects Agency (DARPA), 77

del Alamo, Jesus, 106, 108

DeLauer, Richard, 77–78

Developing world: iLabs in, 107; multiversity in, 109; open-access movement in, 105–6

Digital communications, leadership in, 32

Distance education, 93; for-profit organizations in, 95; MIT task force on, 95–96

Diversity: within American universities, 7–8; institutional commitment to, 23; in public universities, 21–24

Donors, interests in universities, 38, 53. *See also* Philanthropy, educational

Dot-com era, 92; collapse of, 80; economy of, 12; higher education during, 54

DSpace project, 103, 104

Economies, knowledge-based, 53

Education: access to, 20–24, 60, 67–68, 81; business support for, 54; K-12, 55–56

Education, higher: alliance with entrepreneurs, 44; in California, 1–2, 10; during dot-com era, 54; emulation of American system of, 7; geographical variations in, 10–11; globalization of, 70, 81; information technology and, 92–95; innovation in, 36; international students' access to, 74–75; in Internet Age, 91–109; openness in, 4, 47, 70–90; opportunity creation in, 6, 36, 37; philanthropic support for, 8, 50–68, 69; post-9/11, 58; product development in, 80; role of government in, 7, 67; subsidies for, 61; total quality management in, 80; university-industry interaction in, 38–50

Educational technology, 91; profit-generating, 95–96

Eisen, Michael, 103

Eisenhower, Milton, 50

Endowments: donor base of, 53; growing importance of, 51–53; growth of, 53; Japanese, 59; of public universities, 14, 69; of state universities, 52. *See also* Philanthropy, educational

Engineering, financial, 42

Engineering education: African Americans in, 23; changes in, 43–44; intellectual environment of, 3–4

Engineering Experiment Stations, 29

Engineering science, revolution in, 2–4, 98–99

Entrepreneurship: alliance with education, 44; philanthropy from, 55; technological, 42, 43; in United Kingdom, 48

Environment, university/corporate partnerships in, 45

Ethnicity, as factor in admissions, 22

Excellence, academic, 6–9, 36, 60; philanthropic contributions to,

69; populism and, 20; public/private variants in, 19–24

Experiments, repeatability of, 72

Faculty: academic freedom of, 8; competition for, 9; internationalization of, 70; salaries of, 11, 15

Fathom.Com (Columbia University), 93

Federal Acquisition Regulations (FAR), 87

Federal government: Cold War science policy of, 76; control of academic affairs, 67; funding of universities, 12, 13, 15, 24–29; grants from, 61–62; interference with scientific communication, 81, 87–88; partnership with universities, 35; restrictions on openness, 87–89; risk averseness of, 45; support for research, 13, 15, 24–29, 32, 40–41; support for sciences, 8; weapons laboratories of, 76

Fellowships, for graduate students, 56

Financial Accounting Standards Board (FASB), 57

Financial aid, 60–64; alumni support for, 68; bargaining with families in, 66; lawsuits concerning, 64–66; merit-based, 62, 63, 64–68, 69; for minorities, 66; need-based, 62–63, 66, 69; partnerships in, 60; pre-1991 configuration of, 67; purpose of, 60

Foothill-De Anza Community College District (Los Altos, California), 101

Foundations, philanthropy of, 54
Friedman, Tom, 108
Funding, federal, 12, 13, 15, 24–29;
    conditions attached to, 28;
    geographical distribution of, 27;
    reporting requirements for, 28;
    for sciences, 8
Fund-raising, 53–60; private, 14

Garland, James, 18
Gast, Alice, 83
Gel-Man, Murray, 94
Gender, as factor in admissions, 22
Genetics, university research in, 42
Genomes, mapping of, 26
GI Bill, 19
Globalization: effect on innovation
    system, 69; effect on philan-
    thropy, 58–60; of higher educa-
    tion, 70, 81
Global Positioning Satellite (GPS)
    system, 41
Golden, William T., 24–25, 76
Google Print Library Project, 102
Government: role in higher educa-
    tion, 67; role in universities, 4,
    11, 20; and universities' missions,
    38; utilitarian view of, 20. *See also*
    Federal government; States
Governments, local, relations with
    universities, 33–35
Government-University-Industry
    Research Roundtable (GUIRR),
    48
Graduate students: fellowships for,
    56; internationalization of, 70
Grants: federal, 61–62; to K-12,
    55–56; to post-secondary stu-
    dents, 61–62; private, 62; ratio
    to loans, 62

Gray, Paul, 79
Greenspan, Alan, 40
Guichard-Ashbrook, Danielle, 83

Hart, Gary, 73
Hart-Rudman Commission, 73
Harvard University: endowment of,
    14; open access projects of, 102
Hewlett Foundation, 101
Hewlett-Packard Corporation, 103
Higgenbotham, Leon, 66
Higher Education Act, 66
Howard Hughes Medical Institute,
    104
Humboldt University (Berlin), 7

Ideas, free marketplace of, 27, 33
ILab project (MIT), 106–7, 108;
    global participants in, 107;
    Shared Architecture, 107
Immigration and Customs Enforce-
    ment (ICE), 84
Immigration and Nationality Act
    (1952), 82
Immigration policy, post-9/11, 74,
    75, 82
India, research universities of, 91
Indian Institutes of Technology, 9
Industry, American: competitiveness
    of, 30, 39; interest in universities,
    38–50; transformations to, 42–43
Industry, Japanese, competition
    from, 80
Information, scholarly, open flow
    of, 4, 71
Information, scientific: export-
    controlled, 78–79, 87, 88;
    openness in, 72
Information technology: changes
    in, 91; and higher education,

92–95; openness through, 95; as transformative force, 92; university/corporate partnerships in, 45

Innovation: corporate, 43; in higher education, 36; in teaching, 93–94

Innovation system, American, 36, 39–40, 41–42, 50; changes to, 43; effect of globalization on, 69; effect of technological change on, 69

Institute of Electrical and Electronics Engineers (IEEE), 86

Intellectual property: in corporate/university partnerships, 46, 47–48; of meta-university, 93; in open-access movement, 104; openness of, 72; third-party, 96, 104

Internet: development of, 26, 41; empowering properties of, 104; role in scholarship, 4. *See also* World Wide Web

Internet, Age of, 71; higher education in, 91–109

Japan: academic culture of, 59; economic power of, 59; manufacturing revolution in, 28, 42; relations with MIT, 59, 79; technology transfer to, 79–80

Johns Hopkins University, 7

Journals, open-access, 103, 104

JSTOR project, 94–95, 102, 108

K-12 education, philanthropic support of, 55–56

Kennedy, Donald, 77

Kerr, Clark, 70; educational legacy of, 1–2; on multiversity, 2, 91, 108

Knowledge: classified, 72; as deemed export, 78–79, 88

Knowledge, technological, leaking of, 79–80

Knowledge integration communities (KICs), 48–50; goals of, 49–50; stakeholders in, 49

Knowledge transfer, in United Kingdom, 48. *See also* Technology transfer

Laboratories: corporate, 42, 45; web-based, 106–8

Land-grant acts, 10

Learning communities, electronic, 94

Legislators, interests in universities, 37–38

Leverage, in giving, 57

Linux operating system, 109

Los Alamos laboratory, 3

Makere University (Uganda), 107; OpenCourseWare at, 106

Mandela, Nelson, 66

McCracken, Paul, 5

Meta-university, global, 4, 91–109; intellectual property of, 93; philanthropy and, 59; in developing world, 109

Microsoft iCampus initiative, 107

Million Book Project, 102

Minorities, financial aid for, 66

MIT: admissions policy, 22; budget reductions at, 12; community service programs of, 35; corporate partners of, 44–46;

MIT *(continued)*
diversity at, 71; DSpace archive, 103, 104; endowment of, 14; engineering science revolution at, 2–3, 98–99; faculty salaries at, 11; financial aid at, 13, 64–65; iLab project, 106–7; Japanese endowments of, 59; Leaders for Manufacturing (LMF) program, 44; Lincoln Laboratory, 72; as meritocracy, 71; mission statement, 22; Nobel Laureates of, 71; OpenCourseWare Consortium, 100, 106; Open-CourseWare initiative, 95–100, 105, 115n3; in Overlap lawsuit, 64; partnership with Cambridge University, 48, 49; PILOT agreement of, 35; Radiation Laboratory, 3, 98–99; relations with City of Cambridge, 34; relations with Japanese, 59, 79; School of Engineering, 44; security-related research at, 74; Sloan School of Management, 44; sponsored research at, 12; task force on educational technology, 99
Multiversity: contributions to society, 37; intellectual life of, 4; Kerr on, 2, 91, 108

Nanotechnology, 32
NASA, university-based research of, 26
National Academy of Sciences, on national security, 77
National Association of College and University Business Officers (NACUBO), endowment study of, 52, 53

National Defense Authorization Act (2000), 88
National Defense Education Act (NDEA), 56
National Institutes of Health (NIH), funding by, 25–26
National Research Council, 77
National Science Foundation, 25
National security: during Cold War, 26, 76–77, 81; delays in visa processing occasioned by, 82, 85–86; and educational openness, 71, 72, 89–90, 91; National Academy of Sciences on, 77; post-9/11, 74–75, 81
National Security Decision Directive (NSDD) 189, 78, 87
New York Public Library, open access projects of, 102
New York Stock Exchange Index, correlation with philanthropy, 54
Nobel Laureates, at MIT, 71; at University of California, 71
Northwest Ordinance, 10

Obafemi Awolowo University (Nigeria), 107
O'Neill, Gerard, 92
Online Computer Library Center (OCLC), 102
Open-access movement, 102–6; bandwidth in, 104, 105–6; in developing world, 105–6; funding of, 105; intellectual property in, 104; issues facing, 104–6; quality control in, 104, 105; teaching materials in, 105
Open archiving, 102–4

Open courseware, 108; adaptations of, 101; definition of, 100; future of, 101–2

OpenCourseWare (OCW) Consortium, 100, 106

OpenCourseWare (OCW) initiative (MIT), 95–100, 105; alumni reaction to, 116n3; benefits for MIT, 116n3; in China, 101; decision-making for, 115n3; faculty participation in, 115n3; first-mover advantage in, 116n3; mirror sites for, 106; subjects covered by, 97; users of, 97–98, 101, 106

OpenCourseWare (OCW) movement, 100–102; digital publications in, 102–4; tools developed in, 100

Open indexing, 102–4

Openness, educational, 4, 47, 70–90; effect of terrorism on, 4, 70, 73–75; federal restrictions on, 87–89; through information technology, 95; and national security, 71, 72, 89–90, 91; post-9/11, 73–89; scientific, 72; threats to, 70

Openness, of intellectual property, 72

Opportunity, global, 71

Opportunity creation: in higher education, 6, 36, 37; within public universities, 6

Overlap lawsuit, 64–66; appeal of, 65

Pasteur, Louis, 49

Pasteur's Quadrant, 50

Patents: royalties from, 47; universities' approaches to, 48

Payments in Lieu of Taxes (PILOT), 34–35

Pell Grant program, 67–68

Perry, William, 74

Pew Research Center, 84

Philanthropy, educational, 8, 50–68; by alumni, 54; bureaucracy surrounding, 56–57; contribution to excellence, 69; by corporations, 54; from entrepreneurs, 55; future of, 58; governance issues in, 57–58; growing importance of, 51–53; for higher education, 8, 54; by individuals, 56; international, 58–60; leverage in, 57; matching funds for, 57; role of tax laws in, 8; for students, 60–64; transformational significance of, 55. *See also* Endowments

Plagiarism, definitions of, 94

Populism, and academic excellence, 20

Powell, Colin, 86

Print Library Project, 102

Private sector: research and development in, 30; transfer of knowledge to, 33

Privatization, of public universities, 16–19, 52

Professorships, public *versus* private, 16

Publication: electronic, 96–97; open, 102–4; security restrictions on, 75

Public Library of Science (PLoS), 103–4

Public service, universities' commitment to, 9

Race, as factor in admissions, 22–24

Radar systems, development of, 3
Reagan, Ronald: Executive Order
    12356, 77; National Security
    Decision Directive (NSDD)
    189, 78, 87
Research: commercialization of,
    28, 41; corporate support for,
    38–39; economic value of, 47;
    effect of global competition on,
    79–80; export restrictions on,
    78–79, 87, 88; federal support
    for, 13, 15, 24–29, 40–41; global
    models for, 40; independent
    institutes for, 40, 57; indirect
    costs of, 27, 57; *laissez-faire*
    model of, 41; sensitive, 75; sen-
    sitive but unclassified, 77, 78;
    states' support for, 13; student
    access to, 72; teaching and, 8;
    university-industry interaction
    in, 38–50
Research, sponsored: at MIT, 12; at
    University of Michigan, 14
Research and development: corpo-
    rate, 43; effect on state econo-
    mies, 29–33; federal support
    for, 32; international facilities,
    59–60; in private sector, 30;
    security-related, 74; tolerance
    for failure in, 31–32
Researchers, interests in universi-
    ties, 37
Research laboratories, corporate,
    42, 45
Rice, Condoleezza, 87, 89
Roosevelt, Franklin Delano, 24
Rudman, Warren, 73

Sabbaticals, academic, 10
Salaries, faculty, 11, 15

San Diego, leadership in wireless
    communications, 32
Sarbanes-Oxley Act, 57
Scholarship, role of Internet in, 4
Scholarships: need-based, 19; to
    post-secondary students, 61–62
Scientific community, postwar, 24
Search engines, 94
Secrets, military, 76
September 11 attacks: educational
    openness following, 73–89; im-
    migration policy following, 74,
    75, 82; international students
    following, 28, 82–86; national
    security following, 74–75, 81;
    visas following, 82–84; world-
    wide universities following, 85
Sherman Anti-Trust Act, 64
Silicon Valley (California), 30;
    OpenCourseWare at, 97
Social progress, rate of, 92
Society: color-blind, 21, 23; contri-
    butions of multiversity to, 37;
    universities' contributions to,
    58; universities' critique of, 50
Society of Photo-Optical Instru-
    mentation Engineers (SPIE), 77
Sofia (Sharing of free intellectual
    assets) project, 101
Soviet Union: scientific isolation
    of, 72; *Sputnik* launch, 39; tech-
    nological exchanges with, 76;
    technology leaks to, 76
Sputnik, 39
Stanford University: budget reduc-
    tions at, 12; DOD-University
    Forum, 77; open access projects
    of, 102
States: decline in tax bases, 15; eco-
    nomic development by, 30–31;

involvement with universities, 29–33; support for research, 13

Stokes, Donald, 50

Strayer University, 93

Student and Exchange Visitor Information System (SEVIS), 75, 82–83, 84

Students: access to research, 72; competition for, 9, 63, 66; interests in universities, 37; open flow of, 71

Students, international: access to higher education, 74–75; decrease in number of, 85; following 9/11, 28, 82–86; immigrant intent of, 81; Japanese, 79; nonimmigrant status of, 82; tracking of, 75, 82–84; visas for, 75, 81–86

Success, and access to education, 20

Teaching: computer simulations in, 94; innovation in, 93–94; and research, 8; in residential university, 92

Technology: communication, 91; leaks to Soviet Union, 76. *See also* Educational technology; Information technology

Technology Alert List (TAL), 82

Technology transfer: to Japan, 79–80; through knowledgeable workforce, 41; by research universities, 33; role of patents in, 48

Terman, Frederic, 3

Terrorism: effect on educational openness, 4, 70, 73–75; state sponsors of, 82

Thornburgh, Richard, 64

Total quality management, in higher education, 80

Trade protectionism, 79

Truman, Harry, 24; Scientific Research Board of, 76

Tuition: increases in, 13, 68; public *versus* private, 15–16; at state universities, 68

UCLA. *See* University of California (Los Angeles)

United Kingdom, knowledge transfer in, 48

United States: competitive advantage of, 39; foreign public opinion on, 84–85; innovation system in, 39–40, 41–42; science policy in, 8

United States Commission on National Security/21st Century, 73

United States Department of Commerce, export regulations of, 88

United States Department of Defense: research funding from, 25; university affiliations of, 72

United States Department of Energy, funding by, 26

United States Department of Homeland Security, 85

United States House of Representatives: Government Operations Committee, 79; Un-American Activities Committee, 76

United States Justice Department, Overlap lawsuit of, 64–66

United States Office of Management and Budget, Circular A-21, 27

United States Office of Naval Research, 25

United States Treasury Department, Office of Foreign Assets Control (OFAC), 86–87

Universia (Spanish consortium), 101

Universities: academic missions of, 38, 46; construction funding for, 11–12; contributions to society, 58; donors' interests in, 38; enrollment management in, 63–64; federal control of, 67; federal funding for, 12; financial forces affecting, 11–24; flow of information among, 4, 71; industry's interests in, 38–50; intellectual independence of, 50; intellectual property of, 46, 47–48; legislators' interests in, 37–38; partnerships with corporate partners, 44–46; partnerships with states, 29–33; Payments in Lieu of Taxes, 34–35; private funding for, 12, 13; profit-making at, 93; public/private variations in, 11–24; purpose of, 2; relationships with government, 4, 11; relations with local governments, 33–35; researchers' interests in, 37; research-intensive model of, 9; residential, 91–92; role in American innovation system, 40; social contract among, 67; as societal critics, 50; students' interests in, 37; town-gown relations of, 34–35; underground, 97

Universities, American: commitment to public service, 9; diversity within, 7–8; excellence in, 6–9, 19–24, 36, 60; openness in, 70–90

Universities, Ivy League, 7; financial aid at, 65; in Overlap lawsuit, 64, 66

Universities, land-grant, 7; distribution of, 10; public service by, 9

Universities, private: endowments of, 52; enrollment at, 17; expenditures of, 51; revenues of, 51–52; variations from public universities, 11–24

Universities, public: debates concerning, 19–21; diversity in, 21–24; endowments of, 14, 69; enrollment at, 17; expenditures of, 51; flagship, 19; government role in, 20; opportunity creation within, 6, 36, 37; as private corporations, 18–19; private funding at, 14, 52; privatization of, 16–19, 52; revenues of, 51–52; in state economies, 19; variations from private universities, 11–24

Universities, research: of China, 91; federal partnerships of, 35; of India, 91; of mid-twentieth century, 2; of nineteenth century, 7; research and development budgets of, 32; role in economic development, 31; technology transfer by, 33

Universities, state: endowments of, 14, 17, 52; geographical distribution of, 10; social contract of, 18; state government involvement with, 29–33; tuition at, 68; undergraduate education at, 16–17

University of California: Department of Energy laboratories, 72; diversity at, 71–72; as meritocracy, 71

University of California (Berkeley): diversity at, 23; endowment of, 14, 17; state appropriations of, 14, 112n6

University of California (Los Angeles): endowment of, 14, 17; state appropriations of, 112n6

University of Dar-es-Salaam (Tanzania), 107

University of Michigan (Ann Arbor): admissions lawsuit at, 22; budget of, 13–14; endowment of, 14, 17; sponsored research at, 14; state support at, 16, 112n6

University of Oxford, open access projects of, 102

University of Phoenix, 93

University of Texas System, endowment of, 14

University of Virginia: privatization at, 18; state support at, 16

University of Wisconsin, state support at, 16

USA PATRIOT Act (2001), 75

Utah University, Center for Open and Sustainable Learning, 101

Varmus, Harold, 103

Vest, Charles M.: academic career of, 6; and engineering science revolution, 2; MIT presidency of, 5; sabbaticals of, 10; undergraduate education of, 100

Visa CONDOR (national security review), 82

Visa Mantis (national security review), 82, 86

Visas, student, 81–86; delays in, 82; denial of, 75, 81; following 9/11, 82–84

Welcome Trust, 104

Western Governors Conference, 93

West Virginia University, medical school of, 19

Winston, Gordon, 60

World War II, role of radar in, 3

World Wide Web: development of, 92; MIT OpenCourseWare on, 106; open-access materials on, 105; quality control in, 105; role in scholarship, 4. *See also* Internet

World Wide Web Consortium, 42

Text: 10/15 Janson

Display: Janson

Indexer: Roberta Engleman

Compositor, printer, and binder: IBT Global